The
Canoe Guide's
Handbook

The Canoe Guide's Handbook

by Gil Gilpatrick

with photographs by the author

and illustrations by Jon Luoma

DeLorme Publishing Company
Yarmouth, Maine

To Dick Mosher
my lifelong friend, fellow guide, and greatest advocate

Cover design by Jane Crosen
Cover painting by Jon Luoma

ISBN 0-89933-011-8

Contents

Introduction

Today's canoe guide or trip leader is as much a teacher as anything else. Gone are the days when the "sport" sat back and let the guide do all of the work. Most trippers today want the leader to show them how, not do it for them. They want to be participants. In this respect the job is harder now than in times past: while the old-timer took his people through, the modern canoe trip guide must show *them* how to do it. But while the role of guide or leader may have changed, the responsibilities have not.

Any time two or more people get together for a canoe outing, there will be a leader. He or she may be formally appointed—a Boy Scout leader, YMCA leader, summer camp counselor, or church group leader. The person could be the guy or gal in an informal group of friends who is just naturally looked to for leadership. It could be Mom or Dad organizing a family vacation, or it could be someone (like me) making a living, or part of it, by doing what he or she loves most—wilderness canoeing. It is for the folks who find themselves in one of these unenviable, but always challenging, positions that this book is written.

I meet hundreds of these people each summer. Many are experts in their own right, and I never fail to learn something from them. I do not presume to tell them how to conduct their trips, but, as I glean tidbits of information and lore from them, I hope they can find some of my ideas and methods valuable and adaptable to their own outfits. I do know that many of them share a common concern with me, and that is for the safety and well-being of people, especially children, on wilderness canoe trips.

Each year I observe groups canoeing our wilderness waterways who are sadly lacking not just adequate camping gear for a comfortable, enjoyable trip but also adequate safety gear and knowledge of procedures. It isn't uncommon to see young teen-agers with seat cushions for life preservers (legal, but not adequate), and, more often than not, these cushions are stored under the gear in the canoe where they would be of no value if needed. I don't mean to give the impression that the leaders of such groups don't care about their charges. They do! But many of them do not have the experience and know-how to properly outfit a group, and to recognize the dangers that exist in wilderness travel.

I was once asked in an interview what kind of people I met on canoe trips. The expected answer was "all good, likeable people," and that's how I replied. Thinking back on that question, though, I wonder if I should have qualified my answer. I have met people taking canoe trips whom I felt were less than responsible, and I cannot respect people who play games with other people's lives, whether they do it through carelessness or ignorance. Nevertheless, I feel we should take a positive approach to the problem and, whenever possible, prefer education to legislation. I hope this book contributes to that end.

It came as no great surprise to me that the chapter on safety ended up being the largest one in the book. After all, what can be more paramount in a responsible trip leader's mind than the safe return to civilization of everyone in the group? For the sake of organization, the chapter is in two parts: *Preparation*, and *Underway*. Call it an old adage or cliché, but an ounce of prevention *is* worth a pound of cure, and the more you can anticipate at home, the easier things will be underway.

The outfitting, provisioning, and methods that I have laid out are not intended to be the last words on the subject. I am constantly changing, updating, trying to improve and keep up with new products. I'm not too proud to "borrow" an idea from someone if it makes my trips better. By the same token, I hope you will use those ideas of mine that you like, discard the ones you don't, and let me hear about it if you have a better way.

On a wilderness vacation, a safe trip is the obvious priority, but reasonable comfort and enjoyment are important, too. On one of his expeditions in Maine, Henry David Thoreau asked his Indian guide why he did not live off the land. (Thoreau had an idealized picture of Indians traveling through the forest and living off its bounty.) An updated version of the guide's reply is: "No way am I going into the woods without supplies." That's the way I feel, too. It is important to know survival techniques, but I'd rather keep them as a resource in case of an emergency.

I have never really been into eating pine tree parts and the roots and tubers of various plants that grow in the woods, and I am not belittling those who enjoy wild foods, but I would strongly urge that the person responsible for feeding a group of people in the wilderness not depend on their gathering much of their food. Any windfalls along the way can be welcomed and enjoyed, but, from my experience, any initial enthusiasm for foraging daily for wild groceries will probably soon wane.

Where do you draw the line about what to take and what to leave at home? Certainly a canoe party has room for more than the barest of essentials. So, it becomes a matter of priorities of *luxuries*. Which are most important and will do the most for the comfort and well-being of the party? You can see my answer to this in the chapter on checklists. I don't exactly run an austere trip, but I feel we move efficiently and the burden is not overwhelming.

This isn't a beginning canoeist's book. The trip leader should already have a working knowledge of the basic canoeing skills, as well as those involving woodcraft. Where I have touched on these subjects, the purpose has been to help the leader to help others, or to offer tips that I have discovered or "borrowed" from someone else.

There are subjects of vital interest to a canoe trip leader that I have purposely not covered in much depth. One example is the medical section—there are whole books on the subject that do a far better job than I possibly could. Every leader owes it to his or her people to gain as much knowledge as possible in this field and to equip himself or herself accordingly.

Ernest Thompson Seton wrote the following in *The Book of Woodcraft*, published in 1912:

Not long ago a benevolent rich man, impressed with this idea [taking people into the wilderness], chartered a steamer and took some hundreds of slum boys up to the Catskills for a day in the woods. They were duly landed and told to "go now and have a glorious time." It was like gathering up a net full of catfish and throwing them into the woods, saying, "Go have a glorious time."

The boys sulked around and sullenly disappeared. An hour later, on being looked up, they were found in groups under bushes, smoking cigarettes, shooting "craps," and playing cards—the only things they knew.

Thus the well-meaning rich man learned that it is not enough to take men out of doors. We must also teach them to enjoy it.

This is as true now near the end of the century as at its beginning. The leader must not only provide for the physical things to make for a comfortable trip, but also should teach people how to obtain the maximum enjoyment of their wilderness adventure. When asked what that mournful call out on the lake was, don't simply answer "loon," but tell why it fascinates *you*. It will fascinate them, too!

As a leader of a canoe trip, even for a week, you are an authority, host, medic, teacher, etc., as much as a wilderness guide. In showing your people a good time, you'll also show them how to be responsible for themselves—and for their environment—and to appreciate the natural beauty that is still ours to enjoy. An important responsibility rests upon the shoulders of leaders, especially of young people, on wilderness adventures. And if they do the job well, the future of our remaining wilderness areas is assured.

1 Checklists

The problem? To move a group of people and their gear over several hundred miles of road, and to provide for their needs for several days of canoe-camping. Further, to return home with no item left unused except, hopefully, the raincoats, tarp and medical kit. The solution? Check lists! Every single item needed is written on a list, and not checked off until it is packed away, ready to go.

I learned very early in my outdoor wanderings that if I was going to have any success at all I had to get myself organized. Otherwise, I found my mind so occupied with the eager anticipation of the getting there that I did not concentrate sufficiently on the preparation.

My solution was check lists. I don't mean I invented them—but I sure believe in them. I never throw a list away, but alter it and up-date it as needs, materials and equipment change. These small changes are much easier than sitting down and trying to remember everything for a whole new list.

I don't leave out what seems to be obvious, either. Like, canoes! Who's going to forget canoes for a canoe trip? But I list them,

anyway. For one thing, it reminds me to get out and load them—
something I might otherwise put off till the last minute. I admit, I
have never known anyone to forget the canoes, but I have known
hunters to arrive at a hunting camp without a rifle, which would
seem just as obvious.

The lists I use for canoe trips have evolved over many years of
continuous use, along with the evolution of the equipment I use.
Their arrangement suits me and my methods, but I think the
important thing is to get *everything* down on paper. *Then* organize
your lists so that checking items off is easy and natural for you.

Sometimes it is not necessary to list items in detail. An example is
my silverware: When I do up the roll, I know it is all there or I
wouldn't have rolled it. So, I simply list it as "silverware." If your
system is different, you may want to list the items of silverware to
ensure that there will be enough pieces for everyone.

My system consists of six different lists which are shown in this
chapter. Five of the lists are the equipment *I* must pack, and one is
my guests' personal equipment list. Four of my five lists are for the
four different packs that the individual items will go into. The fifth
is a master list of the packs (with their contents as listed per pack),
plus items which do not go into packs.

Individual items are checked off each list as they go into the
appropriate pack. By the time the morning of departure arrives, I
should be down to the master list, having checked all items into
their respective boxes. The master list is to check everything off as
it is loaded into the van and trailer. By disciplining myself to *absolutely not* check an item off until it is packed, there is virtually no
chance of leaving anything behind. Again, being sure it is on paper
somewhere is the key.

I review my lists often for additions and deletions. I watch for
items that never get used, and decide whether or not they should
remain on the list. Even though an item is seldom taken, I might
leave it on a list if I think it would be taken under some circumstances. In this case the list reminds me to *consider* the item; if I don't want
to take it, I just check it off without packing it.

The Kitchen Pack

Check List—The Kitchen Pack
Cook set (includes cups, plates)
Silverware

All of this fits into the kitchen box.

Big spoon
Spatula
Grill
Griddle
Reflector oven
Gas stove
Water pails
Stove fuel
Pot-scrubbing soap pads (2 per day)
Clorox or water treatment tablets
Coffee pot
Candles
Paper towels
Vegetable oil
Coffee
Non-dairy creamer
Sugar
Jam or Jelly
Relish
Mustard

Ketchup
Flour
Salt
Pepper
Extra salt
Boullion cubes
Extra matches
Hand soap
Sponge
Potholders

Wherever I bring the kitchen pack, I have a complete, self-sufficient kitchen. Mostly, it contains the tools needed for meal preparation, but some food items—condiments, coffee, flour, etc.—are also included. Small items are kept in plastic bags so that they won't roll around loose, cluttering things up. The equipment in the pack is sufficient in size and quantity to handle up to 12 people, and I often have this number on a trip. The items on the list of the pack's contents most often handle a party of four to six, but they are adequate for feeding a larger group as well, and extra dishes and utensils are easily added.

As an efficiency item, the pack itself is great—it saves me what could otherwise be endless rummaging for things ("Where *is* that spatula? I *know* I brought it), because all related items are in one place. The pack also provides a clean storage place for kitchen items during the off season.

The kitchen pack I built for my own use is shown in the photo, surrounded by what it usually contains. I have given directions for the pack's construction further on in the book.

Many of the items on the above list explain themselves, but I do have some comments about the major pieces of equipment, and how they are fitted into the pack.

Cook Set: This is a standard aluminum cook set that can be purchased at most outdoor stores. The largest pot is about 3 gallons in capacity, and the rest of the pots nest in it. The whole thing is covered by the frying pan, which has a detachable handle. My set has been used for well over 30 years and is still going strong, so it has proved to be a good long-term investment. The set originally came with six plates (aluminum); I bought enough extras to total 13, and so the set can feed 12, with a spare plate for serving. Fortunately, replacements are easy to come by. (I had to replace a couple of pieces that were lost by some young dishwashers in a white water river—the dishes just disappeared in the rapids.)

Silverware: My silverware roll holds enough forks and spoons for 12 people, plus four or five knives, a can opener, and tongs for handling hot pots and pans. The roll itself was made by my wife. She took a hand towel, folded one end up about 6 inches and sewed the edges, making a 6-inch pouch on one end. On the other end she sewed on a two-foot piece of nylon cord. The whole thing works great! Just dump the silver into the pouch, roll it up, and tie the roll with the attached cord. No drying necessary!

Silverware is easily lost, but I seem to be able to pick up enough pieces, dropped by other campers, to make up for my own losses.

Grill: The grill I carry is just a small thing about two feet long and eight inches wide. I made it by taking three 2-foot pieces of ¼-inch mild steel rod (available from most hardware stores) and welding two 8-inch pieces of the same material across them. It takes up almost no room in the bottom of the box, but comes in very handy if I need to put a pot over the fire. It can be seen standing up behind the kitchen box in the photo.

A self-drying silverware pouch.

Griddle: I use the griddle for pancakes and practically nothing else, but I feel it is worth having along. The material is thick aluminum and it is made to fit the two-burner stove.

Reflector Oven: My favorite cooking tool! I love baking with this little thing, and I enjoy the surprised looks on people's faces when they see a cake or breads baked before the open fire. My oven folds flat and lies on top of the other gear in the box.

Stove: Almost all of my cooking is done on a Coleman two-burner stove. Mine is a Model 425, the smaller of the two-burners available from Coleman. There are times I could use the extra cooking area of a larger stove, but I manage well enough with this one, and I like its compact size.

Water Pails: I buy two of the plastic paint pails sold by hardware stores and paint dealers. They hold about a gallon each and can be nested together. For small groups there are sufficient pots in the cook set to serve as water pails as well as cooking, but with larger parties all of the pots are needed, so additional containers for water are necessary.

Stove Fuel: For everyday use, I keep a spare gallon in the camp tool box.

Pot-scrubbing Soap Pads (Brillo): These cut grease and save heating up dishwashing water. (They also save elbow grease.)

Clorox: This is an inexpensive and effective way to make water safe to drink and to keep dishes germ-free. Two drops per quart will usually be sufficient for clear water; if the water is a little murky use 4 drops per quart. You should get a slight chlorine smell if the amount is correct. If there is no smell, add another drop or two. Double the above amounts for a dish dip. I carry my Clorox in the plastic dropper bottles that food coloring comes in.

Coffee Pot: I refuse to drink instant coffee! A lot of my guests are relieved when they discover I have a percolator in my pack.

Candles: Light, birthdays, fire starting, etc.

A cake rising in a reflector oven. An eagerly awaited treat, especially by youngsters.

Vegetable Oil: For cooking.

Coffee through Flour: These items are stored in square Tupperware containers which fit snugly into a corner of the pack.

The remaining items listed are found in any kitchen, anywhere. You'll certainly have your own ideas about items that you think I am crazy to bother with, there must be some that you don't see how I do without. Do your own thing!

The Tool Pack

Check List—The Tool Pack
Folding saw(s)
Axe
Shovel

Rope
Tarp
Toilet paper
Extra stove fuel
Fly spray
Medical kit
Canoe repair tape
Extra plastic bags
Fire pot
Games
Extra saw blades
Extra tent pegs
Spare stove generator
Tools (screwdriver, pliers, adjustable wrench)

This box seems to catch everything that does not logically (to me at least) seem to belong in any other pack. Most of the contents listed are standard camping items that need no explanation, but I'll make mention of a few of them that may pass along the germ of an idea for you.

Folding saw(s): I take along two or three folding saws. They take up very little space, and they are a big help in getting the wood put up fast. Here's why: I noticed at wood time there was usually a lot of initial enthusiasm, but as the job wore on for fifteen or twenty minutes, interest quickly waned. After too many sessions of finishing up the job myself, I decided I should take advantage of that first spurt of energy by having more tools available. It has worked out well.

Shovel: The shovel is one of those items that I like to be reminded of each trip, but do not always take along. Many of the canoe waterways have out-houses at each campsite because of heavy use. Since the only use I have for the small surplus entrenching tool is latrine digging, I don't take it along on those trips. If there is any doubt, however, it goes.

Fly Spray: This is just the regular household stuff that I like to have along in case someone forgets to zip up his/her tent and finds it full of bugs at bedtime.

Medical Kit: The medical kit in this box is the larger of the two I carry.

Fire Pot: The fire pot is in this pack because there is room for it and, since it is rather dirty on the outside, I'd rather not have it in the kitchen pack. It is an all-purpose pot, used for mixing cold drinks at noon and heating hot water for tea, etc., in the evening. It also serves as a last-minute fire quencher in the morning (after the kitchen is all packed). The list of its uses goes on and on.

Spare Stove Generator: The spare stove generator and the tools needed to change it are a must. The tools are handy for other things, of course, including the changing of spark plugs or shear pins in the outboard, and any of a multitude of things that are super-simple with the right tool, but nigh impossible without.

The Food Packs

Check List—The Food Packs
Meals (from menu)
Snacks
Biscuit mix
Extra coffee
Extra sugar
Extra paper towels
Extra toilet paper

The Cooler
Ice
Meals (from menu)
Butter or margarine

For the most part, these boxes are packed by using the menu as a check list. When I return from the market with the food I break it down into breakfast, lunch and supper, then do any pre-packaging that I feel necessary. Next, I pack the boxes, putting the last day's food in first and working toward the top. If the group will be large, I will use three boxes—one for each meal. I know from experience that the breakfast box will have the most spare space, so I pack the extra items on the food pack list in the bottom of this box before I pack the breakfast meals. If the group is smaller, of course, the meals will be doubled up in one or two boxes.

I think it is important to pack food boxes as soon as possible after I buy the food because everything is fresh in my mind and I know the quantities are correct, having checked them off on the shopping list a little earlier.

Sometimes there is an extraordinary amount of bulky food, such as bread and rolls. Usually at the outset the food boxes will not accommodate these along with the other food, so I'll put the bulky items into a heavyweight trash bag and carry them that way for a day or so until there is some space in the food boxes. The end of the second day out is the longest I generally have to wait to consolidate supplies.

The cooler is loaded with ice and frozen food on the evening before departure. This done, I lower the whole thing into my chest-type freezer for the night. I think if I didn't have a large freezer I would put the frozen items in the chest in the morning and buy my ice en route to the put-in point. However it is done, the main thing is to pack the maximum amount of cold into the cooler and to keep everything under refrigeration until the last possible moment. Every hour *not* exposed to thawing temperature at the start of the trip is an hour longer the ice will last on the other end.

There may be items, such as fresh fruit, that I want to keep cool but not freeze. I note these items at the bottom of the master list so I will not forget to pack them the morning we leave. I don't get too concerned if things like fruit and eggs do not fit in the cooler the first day out because there will be room for them in a day or so, and then they can be left there until the last day, if desired.

The Guest's Equipment List

[NOTE: The following is extracted from my brochure, which each of my guests receives prior to the trip.]

The following is a suggested equipment list. You may add to it if you wish, but bear in mind that you should keep your personal gear as compact as possible. Everything on this list will go into or onto your pack frame and pack bag. There is good reason for everything on this list, so before you decide to omit something give it some thought or ask about it. The following list *includes* clothes worn.

You Will Need
1 pair lightweight boots (well broken in)
1 pair sneakers or moccasins
4 pair socks (athletic sock weight)

4 sets underwear
2 long-sleeved shirts
2 long pants
1 strong belt
1 lightweight windproof jacket
1 sweater or sweatshirt
1 raincoat
1 hat with brim
1 toothbrush
1 soap
1 toothpaste
1 towel
1 swimming suit
2 sticks or bottles insect repellent
1 warm sleeping bag
2 large handkerchiefs
1 pack frame with bag
1 flashlight
1 set extra batteries
1 cup (metal or plastic with handle)
1 laundry soap
1 foam pad or air mattress

Optional
Camera and film
Medicine if required
Spare eyeglasses if needed
Pocket knife
Snacks
Fishing gear (license needed)
Shaving gear
Reading material

Remember, you are going to live out of your pack for an extended period of time, so give some thought to packing so as to prevent daily unpacking and repacking. I like to use packages within the pack: I take appropriately sized plastic bags and put related items together in them. The plastic slides in and out easily without disturbing the rest of the pack, and the plastic helps keep things dry if the pack gets wet. Of course, items that are used most often should be near the opening, etc. Keep the raincoat handy at all times—you won't be sorry!

* * *

This list is meant to be the minimum, and it is anticipated that each person will have his or her own idea of what is "needed" besides the items I have listed as necessary. This is to be expected, and is okay as long as the inexperienced person doesn't get too carried away.

I recall a boy on a 225-mile canoe trip I guided a few years back. He was enthusiastic about fishing, and on a shorter trip the previous year he had met some fisherman who convinced him he needed live bait to be a successful summertime trout fisherman. He showed up for the long trip, three weeks with many portages, with a live bait trap that was about three feet long and ten or twelve inches in diameter—this in addition to his regular complement of fishing gear, which was considerable. In a weak moment I allowed him to take it all and he finished the trip with it, but everyone in the group had some choice words for the thing at one time or another. He is a young man now, and we see each other occasionally. This incident is always good for a laugh.

Personal Equipment List

Check List—My Personal Equipment
1 boots
1 shoes
1 extra laces
4 socks
4 shorts
4 tee-shirts
2 long sleeved shirts
2 pants
1 jacket
1 belt
2 handkerchiefs
1 bathing suit
1 rain suit
1 hat
1 towel
1 washcloth
1 toothbrush
1 toothpaste
1 soap
1 razor ard blades
1 shave cream
1 laundry soap

1 medical kit (small)
1 sewing kit
Safety pins
Pocket knife
Fly dope
Nylon rope
Compass
Maps
Matches
Lighter
Flashlight
Camera equipment
Notebook
Glasses and case
Plastic bags
Sleeping bag
Sleeping pad
Emergency blanket
Pack frame
Canteen
Extra batteries
Cup
Hunting knife
Check book
Cash
Permits

Fishing gear
Vest
Rod
Reels
Line dressing
Fly dressing
Fishing Flies
Leaders
Tip-its
Clippers
Net

My list is just an extention of the one I give my guests. Most of the items here that do not appear on the other list are to help me to do my job.

The small medical kit in my pack holds the usual supplies like band-aids, antiseptic salve, aspirin, etc. My pack is always handy, and it saves digging out the big kit for minor things.

For an emergency blanket I carry one of those marketed as Space Blankets. They are compact and warm. I have never had to use one on a canoe trip, but I consider it good insurance to have along. It can substitute for a sleeping bag in an emergency; a friend used mine once on a hunting trip when his bag was lost. They are kind of clammy because they do not breathe, but they *are* warm.

Most of my trips are during the summer months, so the lists are designed for that season. For an early or late trip I add a few heavier items like a jacket, sweater, and other appropriate clothing.

Everything except my camera equipment will go into or onto my pack frame. If I limited myself to one camera I could get it into the pack too, but since I carry two cameras and several lenses, I need a separate box.

This is all of the camping gear for a party of 10. This plus personal packs is all that has to be lugged ashore each day.

THE CANOE GUIDE'S HANDBOOK

Within fairly obvious limits, the key word in the personal equipment lists is "personal." This is where each person takes along his or her own important items. Maybe it will not even appear on the list, but it will surely get into the pack. Some things do not have to be written down, I guess: these are things important only to the person involved. I know that it would be a rare trip that did not find a novel tucked away into my pack for those windbound days, or whatever. Still, I never got around to adding "book" to my list; I doubt that I will ever need to.

The Master List

Check List—The Master List
Canoes
Paddles (3 per canoe)
Bailers
Life jackets (1 per person)
Tents
Poles
Motor
Motor gas
Motor bracket
Cooler
Kitchen pack
Food packs
Tool pack
Personal packs
Other:

_____
_____
_____
_____
_____
_____

When all items are checked off on all the other lists, I am down to the master list. The main purpose of this list is to check the boxes and packs onto the van or trailer, and to remind me of the items that do not get packed into a container. It is the last thing I look at before heading out for the river.

The bottom of this list is where I write anything that I want to be sure not to forget at the last minute. Here I might list eggs, fruit, bread or any unusual item that may be unique to that particular trip. Obviously, items like canoes, paddles, etc. do not have to be left until the morning of departure to be loaded, so they will be checked off earlier, but this list represents the final countdown.

When the master list is completely checked off, I kiss my wife goodbye and we are on our way. No need to stop for one last look around. No need to stop and think if I may have forgotten something. No worrying all the way to the river whether something I could not remember packing is there. *I know! I know* everything we will want or need was on a list. *I know* I checked everything on the lists into their containers and then onto the transport. It is a great feeling to start off with that kind of confidence!

2 Provisioning the Trip

Early canoe travelers had to provision themselves either by living off the land or by taking food with them, or a combination of the two. Most chose the latter. The take-along food provided the barest of sustenance, and fish and game filled their bellies when the opportunity presented itself. Remember, these people, Indian or white, were not out for the pleasure of it; they had to get somewhere. The take-along food was essential for rapid travel. Otherwise, much valuable time would have been spent searching for food.

The *voyageurs* who canoed for a living in the fur trade had gigantic appetites. Records show their daily ration was 10 pounds of salmon, 15 pounds of whitefish, or three pounds of pemmican. This is a tremendous amount of food, but these traders expended a huge amount of energy, paddling 18 hours a day, with 60 paddle strokes per minute. Amazingly, they made their portages at a trot, carrying two and even three 90-pound bundles at a time.

Lest you yearn for the "good old days," read the following quote from H. M. Robinson's *The Great Fur Land: or Sketches of Life in the Hudson's Bay Territory*, published in 1879:

...take the scrapings from the driest outside corner of a very stale piece of cold roast beef, add to it lumps of tallowy, rancid fat, then garnish all with long human hairs, on which string pieces, like beads upon a necklace, and short hairs of dogs or oxen, or both, and you have a fair imitation of common pemmican. Indeed, the presence of hair in the food has suggested the inquiry whether the hair on the buffaloes from which the pemmican is made does not grow on the inside of the skin. The abundance of small stones or pebbles in pemmican also indicates the discovery of a new buffalo diet heretofore unknown to naturalists.

One thing you can say about provisioning in the "good old days" is that it was kept simple: a bag of pemmican or a side of bacon and a bag of beans was all the planning required.

You, the modern day trip leader, are faced with the opposite problem. So many practical choices are available that it is often difficult to determine what is best to use and how best to use it. You must find the answers to questions such as: How much? Traditional or non-traditional? To refrigerate or not?, and many more. Then, too, unless you have an unlimited budget, cost has to be considered.

The purpose of this chapter is not to give you recipes and tell you what you should take for food. There are already books on the market that do this, and some do it very well. What I have tried to do here is to present a logical and well-tested method of determining the foods that best suit the needs of the group. I do confess to slipping in hints and tips here and there that I have tried and found especially good. Further, I plead guilty to the unabashed appropriation of some of these from my wife, my fellow guides, and even my friends.

The Menu and Shopping List

"How do you know what to take for food?" or "How do you know how much food to take?" One or both of these questions are asked of me over and over in discussing the organization of canoe trips. While I consider provisioning the hardest part of putting a trip together, it becomes manageable when the task is broken down to a day-by-day, meal-by-meal basis. This takes care of the "what" (menu) and the even more difficult decision of "how much" (list).

The trip leader planning for his or her own family has first-hand knowledge of likes and dislikes, as well as a good idea of the quantity likely to be consumed. Planning food for strangers or even friends is not so easy. You must depend on good judgment and common sense, and draw on any experience you may have. The old saying "You can't please 'em all" holds true. You may have no way of knowing how many really big eaters will be along. However, if you choose good nutritious food that *you* like, and in a reasonable quantity, most people will be happy and satisfied. If you try to poll the group and come up with a menu to please everyone, the job becomes impossible.

I half-jokingly tell people that I take food that *I* like; that way, I'm sure at least *one* person on the trip will be satisfied. This always gets me a dirty look from my wife, but I'm really not that selfish about it. However, unless you have unusual tastes in food it is reasonable to assume that others will like the same menu, at least to some degree. For sure, find out if anyone has a problem with certain foods, but don't worry about trying to serve everyone's favorites.

The Menu

The first step in the provisioning process is to prepare a menu such as the one shown on the next page. I have used this menu, with some variation, many times for groups ranging in size from 4 to 12 people. Only the quantities on my shopping list have to be changed to accommodate various-sized groups.

I like to use the days of the month on the menu. I carry it with me on the trip, and it helps me keep track of the date; it is easy to remember what was eaten the day before. Keeping track of the date may not seem important or in keeping with the carefree spirit of a canoe trip, but the leader isn't afforded this carefree luxury. If your group is scheduled to meet transportation at a certain time and place, it would be embarrassing, and troublesome, to arrive at the appointed place a day early or late.

In writing items down on the menu, try to think of everything in the food line that will be needed to put that meal before your guests. If you don't have things like salt and pepper on another list somewhere, then get it down on the menu so you won't forget it.

I use three basic breakfasts and just keep rotating them. Even if each is prepared exactly the same way each time, this repetition is not too frequent and does not become tiresome. However, it is seldom necessary to serve them the same way more than once.

The eggs can be fried, scrambled, boiled or poached. The pancakes can be served plain or with freshly picked blueberries, raspberries, strawberries, etc., depending on the season. Dried fruit can also be

Sample Menu
Murphy Party
Eight people July 21 - 28

Day	Breakfast	Lunch	Supper
21		Bag lunch 9 people	Hot dogs, rolls, mustard, relish drink, dessert
22	Eggs, toast, butter, jam, coffee, hot chocolate	Crackers, cheese, drink, candy	Hamburger Helper, Hamburger, vegetables, biscuits, drink, dessert
23	Pancakes (mix), syrup	Crackers, Peanut butter, drink, candy	Spaghetti, spaghetti sauce, hamburger, biscuits drink, dessert
24	Oatmeal, dried milk, toast	Crackers, meat spread, drink, candy	Macaroni & cheese, biscuits, vegetables, drink, dessert
25	Eggs, etc.	Crackers, cheese, etc.	Hamburger Helper, Hamburger, vegetables, biscuits, drink, dessert
26	Pancakes, etc.	Crackers, peanut butter, etc.	Beef stew, biscuits, drink, dessert
27	Oatmeal, etc.	Crackers, meat spread, etc.	Scalloped potatoes, Spam, biscuits, vegetables, drink, dessert
28	Eggs, etc.	Crackers, cheese, etc.	

used with pancakes. The oatmeal is the most likely of the three to be dull, so I always have raisins along to spark it up a bit, and, of course, the fresh berries will do wonders for it, too. I always plan so that the oatmeal breakfast has the least number of repetitions, for it is usually least popular.

Some items on the menu are intended to be used at some other, unspecified, time during the trip, so I keep this in mind when figuring the quantities of these items. Cooking oil, for example, will be used often, but as long as it is written down once and an adequate quantity is recorded on the list, it isn't necessary to repeat it. The same goes for coffee, hot chocolate, etc.

Like the breakfasts, three different lunches seem adequate for variety. They are laid out as shown in the menu for planning purposes, but in actual use I have found it best to put out some of each item with each meal. This way, everyone gets to eat his/her preference, or a little of each, every day. It works out well. Otherwise, suppose some person really hates peanut butter: besides dreading peanut butter day, that person would probably fill up on plain crackers, leaving the rest of the group with too few of them to spread their peanut butter on.

Speaking of crackers, these work out better than bread because they are sealed in plastic and will not get stale and spoil. There are a variety of kinds and flavors of crackers available, and they make a light but satisfying lunch.

The candy I use comes in plastic bags, usually labelled "fun size" (my daughter says they should be a lot bigger to be really fun), each bag containing 20 to 25 small candy bars. For large groups these can be packed as is and divided on the river bank. If the group is small, I break them down into smaller packages while packing.

My supper meals have been selected from many experiments for variety, adaptability to different sizes and types of groups, and for ease of preparation in camp. On most trips I carry a cooler with ice, and this menu was designed with this in the plan, but if I cannot take an ice chest then I just make a few changes in the menu. This isn't as hard as it may seem. Here's how I would go about it:

The first meal on the menu is no problem; it will keep. The second supper is Hamburger Helper. It has only one item that has to be refrigerated—the hamburger. I would cook the meat at home and pack it along with the rest of the meal. (Cooked meat will not spoil in such a short time.) In the third supper it is again the hamburger, this time for the meat sauce, that is the only item needing special care. In cool weather it can be handled the same way as the Hamburger

A large flat rock in Allagash Lake was the lunch area this day.

Helper meal, but if the weather is hot I would not chance it. Rather, I would buy some freeze-dried meat and rehydrate it when needed for the sauce. The macaroni and cheese meal—no problem. As for the second Hamburger Helper meal (it comes in a variety of flavors), use freeze-dried meat again. Beef stew can be taken in the can. The scalloped potatoes and Spam meal—no problem.

The vegetables for a no-cooler trip can be canned, or freeze-dried, but I have found a better way. I pick up a dried vegetable soup mix at the supermarket for a vegetable—it goes great!

If you object to carrying home a few jars and cans, you can rely more heavily on the dried camping foods and virtually eliminate them. However, I find that a few containers are very manageable, and may even come in handy. I just wash them out and slide them to the bottom of the food boxes where they remain until I get home.

The menu shown isn't meant to show what you should take, but is to help you to *determine* what to take. Many of the supper meals I use either are, or closely approximate, some of the meals my wife serves at home. She doesn't use Hamburger Helper, but the different flavors of this product are somewhat like some of her casseroles. This is the way to start: Write down what you like, and then adapt and adjust what is available, easy, and practical for camp use.

I try for as much variety as possible in my supper meals, but as few as five basic suppers can be rotated without getting tiresome if a little ingenuity is used during preparation. I have done this when I wanted to travel as simply and as lightly as possible. With the great choices available today from the supermarket and from camp food suppliers, there is no need for anyone to serve tiresome, unattractive food in camp.

The Shopping List

Once the menu is complete and you are satisfied with it, make up the shopping list. This is decision time again: "How much do I need?" If you lack experience in amounts for any particular food, ask someone who cooks for a family how much they use. I often consult my wife in this area when trying something for the first time. Be sure to add extra for that outdoor appetite, and if you will have teen-agers along, add some more. You can go by the number of servings indicated on a package, but for camping purposes you will usually need half again to twice as much as recommended on the label.

Shopping List—Murphy Party
Eight People—8 days

2 lg. sandwich meat (1st day lunch)
2 pkgs. sliced cheese (1st day lunch)
5 cans powdered drink mix (one for 1st day lunch, the rest for supper meals)
2 pkgs. brownie mix (1st day lunch)
2 doz. hamburger rolls
2 doz. hot dog rolls
2 lbs. onions
1 small jar mustard
1 small jar relish
7 desserts (variety)
5 doz. eggs
5 loaves bread
2 lbs. margarine

1 large jar jam
1 large bottle vegetable oil (plastic bottle if available)
3 lbs. coffee
2 large boxes hot chocolate mix (add only water)
11 boxes crackers (variety of flavors)
6 cheese (8-10 oz. blocks)
14 2 qt. pkgs. powdered drink mix (for lunches)
7 pkgs. candy (small bars; for lunches)
6 Hamburger Helper (2 flavors, 3 pkgs. for each meal)
9 lbs. hamburger
4 vegetables
2 pkgs. Bisquick
2 boxes pancake mix (complete, just add water)
2 large bottles pancake syrup (plastic bottles)
5 lbs. peanut butter
3 lbs. spaghetti
3 large jars spaghetti sauce
1 small box oatmeal
1 small box dried milk
1 box raisins
8 cans meat spread
4 boxes macaroni & cheese mix
3 large cans beef stew
3 pkgs. scalloped pototoes mix
3 cans Spam

* * *

2 gallons stove fuel
18 Brillo pads
2 rolls paper towels
1 small jar non-dairy coffee creamer
1 box boullion cubes
2 rolls toilet paper (hard rolls)
1 pkg. large plastic bags (trash bags)
7 snacks (cake mixes, popcorn kernels, other)
1 pkg. candles
3 blocks of ice
Motor gas and oil

It pays to have extras of some items. If you bring extra hot
chocolate mix, everyone can have a cup after a long cold day of
paddling in the rain. Extra biscuit mix takes up very little room in
the food box, but an extra batch would be helpful in stretching a

meal that happens to come up a little short on something; another biscuit with jam or peanut butter will help fill up that hollow leg. These and other contingencies are impossible to plan into the menu, but are very easy to allow for, if you think about it. Peanut butter is my "emergency rations"—I always take plenty. It can be used to fill out any meal or served as a filling, nutritious snack in-between.

Once every item on the menu has been listed with a quantity added to it, I go over my check lists for items that I have to buy for the trip, such as paper towels, toilet paper, soap pads, etc. With all needed items listed, one trip to the market does it all.

Traditional vs. Non-traditional Foods

I have at times relied quite heavily on dried and freeze-dried foods for canoe trips. There are a number of advantages to these foods, and I still find them useful from time to time; usually, however, I find almost everything I need on well-stocked supermarket shelves.

Dried food is easiest to use when pre-packaged (either by you or the manufacturer). This makes meal preparation a cinch—you just pull out the designated bag for the particular day and follow the instructions for preparation.

Dried food weighs a fraction of the original food, so you do not have to carry around a lot of water. This makes a lot of sense; there's no shortage of water on a canoe trip. I believe most of the name-brand dried foods will provide a nutritionally balanced diet if the foods are carefully selected and prepared according to the directions.

I would say that my own experience with dried foods has been positive, and I can only think of two reasons that I do not regularly use them. The first is cost: You have to pay the bill for that expensive processing, especially the freeze-drying. If you buy the pre-packaged meals, then you have to pay for the meal planning and packaging that has been done for you.

The second reason is that, even with a good variety of entrees, there seems to be a sameness in taste after a few days. This is a hard thing to describe, and some people seem to notice it more than others. I've never really considered it a serious drawback, but some do. It *is* a factor to be considered. I've never had a lot of real complaints, but it has been mentioned by several of my guests from time to time.

I get everything possible from the grocery store, and when there is nothing there to fill a particular need I rely on a freeze-dried item. Keep an open mind whenever you're in the supermarket. Be constantly alert for items, especially new items, that will be tasty, nutritious, and easy to prepare. The less you have to add to a prepared mix, the easier it is for you. The ideal is to only need to add water. There are a lot of mixes on the shelves that meet this ideal.

The kind of trip being undertaken has the greatest bearing on what can be taken for food. If the trip is relatively easy with no long portages, then weight, within reason, is not a problem and there is no reason why you should not eat essentially what you would eat at home. You can take along a cooler with ice and enjoy fresh foods with very little inconvenience.

On the other hand, a trip that will involve difficult carries around rapids, between watersheds and over sundry obstacles should be planned for efficient portaging. Trudging over a two-mile portage for the third time with a cooler containing ice that will eventually melt away does not seem productive, somehow. (This is my view; yours may be different.) I have met people on trips who carried along lawn chairs. To me, this seemed a useless luxury, but to them they were an essential part of their gear, and they would sooner part with their camp stove than their chairs. To each his own.

If a cooler will be taken, the choice of food is almost unlimited, and your party can enjoy all of the fresh fruits, vegetables and meats that you have room to pack. With careful planning, this can be quite a lot.

In packing the cooler, I start out by freezing everything that can be frozen and putting these items in with the ice. These frozen foods serve as extra ice, and will help make the blocks of ice last that much longer. Except for the eggs, almost everything can be frozen: margarine, cheese, meats, entrees, etc. For the first day or two you will have to plan ahead if you want to use a frozen item, just as you would if it were in the home freezer. The main idea is to pack as much cold (frozen food) into the cooler as possible.

Don't worry about the fresh eggs. They keep well without refrigeration, and in a day or two there will be space in the cooler for them, anyway.

I have managed to finish a ten-day trip with remnants of ice still in the cooler. To do this requires careful handling, however. Only you should open the lid, and then only after carefully considering everything that is needed so that all can be quickly gathered up at a single opening. Everyone should be made to understand the importance of leaving the cooler closed.

When in camp, keep the cooler in the shade. In the canoe it is hard to prevent the sun from beating down on it, but provide as much shade as possible. Drain the water as often as is practical—at least twice a day. That water is heat; otherwise it would still be ice. Get rid of it.

For a really long trip, consider using dry ice. It can either be used by itself or with wet ice, the idea of the combination being that the wet ice takes over when the dry ice is gone. Dry ice is 106 degrees *below* zero Farenheit, so everything in the cooler will be very solid as long as any of it remains. You have to remember to plan an even longer thawing time because the food will be 106 degrees colder than it would be from your home freezer. Dry ice is expensive, but can be very worthwhile in some circumstances.

On trips where portages will be long and hard, I take a lesson from our brothers and sisters in wilderness travel: the backpackers. Those folks have traveling light down to a science, and while a canoeist does not really need to go to the extremes of the hikers, he or she should certainly listen to, read and learn from them. After all, besides a canoe, paddles, and a life perserver, what does a canoeist really need that a backpacker does not carry? The answer is nothing, of course, so it is safe to say that everything else besides these items and a backpack are luxuries.

One of the advantages of canoe travel is that some luxuries are possible, and each individual decides which are important for a particular trip. This brings me back to the cooler. If it seems worthwhile, I take it. If I think it will be more trouble than it is worth, I leave it at home and plan my food accordingly.

If you want help with good non-refrigerated meals for canoeing, I recommend the book: *The Complete Pack Provisioning Book* by Nancy Jack, published by Contemporary Books, Inc., 180 North Michigan Avenue, Chicago, Illinois 60601. This well-researched book is a valuable tool in selecting lightweight food either from traditional sources or from camping food suppliers.

Meal Preparation

I have so often watched what appears to be a leaderless group at mealtime. Eventually someone cries out, "Mashed potatoes ready," and each person files by for a portion of mashed potatoes and goes off to eat them. In a while, someone else yells, "Hamburgers done," and everyone picks up one shriveled-up hamburger, with the promise of another to come. This goes on and on, one item at a time, until everything is doled out and eaten, and then each person is left to his or her own devices for cleaning up his/her dishes. (I suppose some luckless individual is left with the job of scrubbing out the cooking dishes, although I admit I have never learned just how this chore is handled.) There *is* a better way, and with a little organization you can produce a coordinated, civilized meal.

With the planning and pre-portioning taken care of, the hardest part of meal preparation should already be done before you leave home. Where applicable, the correct amounts should have been measured out. If you've written your meal plans on a menu, all you need do is consult it to determine everything needed. Finally, you should have with you the necessary tools and equipment to properly lay out the complete meal.

If the leader takes pride in the meal and cares about what he is offering his or her guests, those guests will sit down and eat a well-balanced, attractive meal that is hot, delicious and filling. It does not take an army of helpers to put on such a meal—just careful planning and some thinking ahead. I have fed hundreds of meals to groups of 4 to 12 people without ever having to serve cold or burnt-on food. I have done it alone, although volunteers are always welcomed and usually available.

Although the menu is a valuable tool both before and during the trip, don't be a slave to it. Be flexible enough to take advantage of fresh fish, wild fruit, or other windfalls of food. If an unexpected catch of fish will fit better into one meal than another, then go ahead and switch the menu around.

I use two sources of heat for my meal preparation: the two-burner gasoline-burning Coleman stove and the campfire. Most of my cooking is done on the stove; the fire is used for baking with a reflector oven, for warming already-cooked foods and finishing up with others. I always carry along that old kettle I call the fire pot, or the "black pot." This is kept on the fire for a continuous source of hot water as needed by me or my guests.

Mealtimes

Meal preparation for the day starts with breakfast. I am always up at least an hour before my guests. In this time I perk the coffee, build the campfire, heat water and lay out all of the necessary ingredients for the breakfast of the day. This takes maybe 30 to 45 minutes, and I appreciate the remaining time for quiet solitude with a cup of coffee in front of the fire.

Cleaning fiddleheads. Take advantage of wild foods, but don't depend on them.

At the agreed-upon time I wake everyone up, and after a short wait (to allow time for face washing and other personal hygiene) I start breakfast cooking. Since the coffee is already done and hot water is ready for hot chocolate, the total time required for breakfast, beginning to end, is not more than 30 minutes.

With breakfast over, my guests return to their tents to roll up their gear and take down their tents. With a small group, I would probably wash the dishes and then do the same. With larger groups, the dishwashing chores are almost always shared.

Dishwashers work in pairs. If they are from the same tent, you can save time by having them roll up their gear and place it outside the tent before starting the dishes. Then, the first people finished with their own tent can strike the dishwashers' tent.

Once the dishes are done, I can pack up the kitchen in less than 5 minutes and have it on shore ready to put into the canoe.

With all this stressing of timing, it may seem as though I'm always hurrying my guests, but it isn't that way at all. Setting up and breaking down camp is not fun; it is work. The sooner it is over and done with, the sooner everyone can get on with what they are there for: canoeing. The leader can, by subtle urging, suggesting, and example, keep everything moving smoothly and quickly to get the group onto the water. I have seen groups without a strong leader spend two to three hours eating and breaking camp. What's the fun in that? I have had groups that could be on the water *one hour* after they crawled out of their sleeping bags. I admit, this is faster than

A lakeside kitchen with driftwood furniture. Here, the food boxes doubled as a serving line for a party of 12.

THE CANOE GUIDE'S HANDBOOK

usual, but one hour and fifteen minutes is normal, and any group that takes more than an hour and a half is a slow one indeed.

Although lunch requires no great amount of preparation, this meal is a lot easier to fix if everything involved is put together before you head down the river in the morning. Then, all that is necessary at lunchtime is to mix up the drink and lay the food out on the riverbank for everyone to help themselves.

The supper meal is the largest of the day and the one by which the leader is judged as to his or her culinary abilities. Again, with everything planned ahead of time, there should be no problems. You can even cheat by having some help at home with advance preparation.

Right here is a good place to emphasize an important point that applies to the preparation of any meal: cleanliness. A lot of jokes are made about how everything tastes good outdoors, including the dirt and so on and so forth, but the fact is that no one appreciates dirt, nor should they have to put up with it in or around their food. I keep a bar of soap in my kitchen pack, and before I start any meal I make a point of using it. It isn't necessary to make a big production of this washing up, but it doesn' hurt for the guests to see you do it, either. I feel this is one of the most important "little things" that the leader can do.

I usually start puttering around my kitchen about an hour before supper time. I fill my stove fuel tank, get the water I will need, start the coffee, start water heating for cooking, if needed, and build the fire. Guests enjoy an early cup of coffee while waiting for supper, as I do while I am preparing it.

If I am having biscuits with the meal, I make sure to get them into the reflector oven and in front of the fire while the rest of the supper is cooking on the camp stove.

When supper is ready and while everyone is eating, I have water heating for dishwashing. This water may be heated either on the stove or over the fire. By the time everyone has finished eating and the dishes are washed, the water is boiling and ready for a hot rinse.

Clean-up

My dishwashing system is very simple. I take soap-filled steel wool pads (Brillo or SOS), one pad for each meal. The dishes are washed in cold water with the pad; make sure your dishwashers are careful to rinse off all traces of soap. (The dish should feel squeaky-clean when rinsed.) When all the dishes are washed and cold-water-rinsed, rinse them again with hot water.

This method works perfectly for ninety-five percent of the meals served. The only time you'll encounter trouble is when you've served something extremely greasy, such as bacon. This causes more grease on the dishes than the soap pad can handle in cold water, and greasy dishes will result. When I have this situation, I just heat up two batches of hot water and wash in hot water as well as rinsing with it.

If you as leader do not do the dishes yourself, at least do the hot rinse so that you can check them for cleanliness and for grease. Remember, you are responsible. Your guests are expecting you to show them how to have a good time. They won't enjoy themselves much if they spend a day or two with cramps and diarrhea.

Snacks

The final bit of food preparation I do for the day is to make a snack of some kind. This is usually a cake baked in the reflector oven (the favorite), but could be popcorn or a pudding or even some dried fruit if a cold snack is desirable.

For camping use, the cake mixes (like Snackin' Cake) that need only water are what I find best. Then, all you need to do is mix the contents of the box in the cook set frying pan with a cup of water and put it in the oven. They only difficult part of cake baking is leveling the oven so that the batter doesn't run to one side of the pan. All you can do is eyeball its position and make adjustments to the oven by propping it with little stones here and there, then hope for the best.

Very often someone in the group has a birthday while we are out. To prepare for this possibility I always take along an extra cake mix, a can of prepared frosting and a candle of some kind—everything needed for a two-layered birthday cake—and we have a party that is always very special to the person being honored because of where it is taking place. The group often gets into the spirit by donating their lunchtime candy bars for the occasion, and often they fashion some sort of gift from materials at hand.

If there is no birthday, I make the layer cake on the last evening out to celebrate our last night together around the campfire. Little things like this take up very little space in the food box but a lot of space in people's memories.

Bad Weather Meals

Rainy days present problems for everyone on a canoe trip. If it is a prolonged rain everyone will, *at best*, be damp and cold at the end of the day. At worst, they will be soaking wet and cold. The leaderless group in this situation will, more often than not, grab whatever can be eaten as is and crawl into their tents and hope for better times to come.

It is up to the leader to put forth that extra effort to see that everyone has hot food, hot drink and a nice warm fire. While everyone else is setting up the tents, you should be getting the fire going and preparing hot drinks. These two things, more than anything else I know, will boost morale on a cold wet day. It isn't just the hot fire, food and drinks; it is the fact that you are in control and can handle any situation you are likely to encounter. Their confidence in you goes up with their spirits.

Some Mealtime Tips

First Lunch: The first lunch of the trip is a bag lunch that is made up at home. This way we can eat at noon whether we are still en route to the put-in point, at the put-in point, or somewhere down the river. There will thus be no need to dig out food boxes which are liable to be under other dunnage, especially if we are still on the road.

The First Supper: The first supper is kept simple. Face it—if any meal of the trip will be hectic, it will be this one. Everyone is somewhat disorganized this first day, and any number of unforeseen things could cause you to get into camp late. Why hassle with a complicated meal when almost everyone likes hot dogs and rolls? Each person roasts his/her own—all you have to do is build a fire and lay everything out.

Cold Drinks: To prepare cold drinks, I buy the already-sweetened mix that just has to be added to water. I buy it in pre-measured (two-quart) packages for lunches so that all I have to do is measure the water and stir in the mix. For supper, I use the mix which comes in the more economical cans that make two gallons of drink. (In camp, measuring the mix as well as the water is no bother.)

Hot Drinks: For hot drinks, I carry coffee and tea for adults and hot chocolate for everyone who might want some. I also keep some boullion cubes tucked away for an emergency pick-me-up. I carry more of all hot drink mixes than I expect to use, for a good hot drink is a great morale lifter whenever someone (or everyone) is cold and wet. And, this situation is not unheard-of on a canoe trip.

Desserts: I keep desserts quite small and simple—usually a package of cookies for each supper meal. There are two reasons for this: First, I usually bake a fresh snack later on each evening. Second, my main course is designed to be large and filling; most people don't feel like eating a large dessert.

Pre-package: Whenever possible, I pre-measure and pre-package at home. It is easier to do there, and it saves taking along the part of a package that will not be used. For example, I have oatmeal on the menu for two mornings. I do not take a box of oatmeal and a box of dried milk; instead, I measure the required amount of oatmeal into a couple of plastic bags, and include in each a bag of pre-measured dried milk, along with a note reminding me how much water to add. Then I seal them up, one breakfast meal per bag. These materials take up very little space that way. (Raisins are taken for oatmeal, but in a box because they can also be used as a snack food if needed.)

The Cooler: When a cooler is taken, wet meal components like spaghetti sauce can be portioned, per meal, in heavy plastic bags and frozen. If, in preparing your spaghetti sauce, you've already scrambled the hamburger and mixed it in, all that you need to do when spaghetti day rolls around is heat up the sauce and cook the the spaghetti. Any meal featuring a sauce can be handled this way. The cans and jars (or saucepans used in cooking) can be left at home, and the extra cold mass in the cooler helps to make the ice last longer.

Eggs: I always take along a few extra eggs. This allows for breakage, and they come in handy for impromptu baking in camp.

Pancake Mix: Pancake mix is available as a complete mix, and all you have to add is enough water to give the batter the consistency you desire. (You could even make your own mix—use powdered eggs.)

Containers: Whenever you have a choice, buy what you need in plastic or paper packages. These can burn in the campfire and will leave you with that much less material to carry out.

Wild Fruit: If you are lucky enough to have an energetic bunch of berry pickers, you should be prepared to take advantage of a bonanza of fresh fruit. Combine the following ingredients needed to make a wild fruit cobbler, and keep the mixture tucked away somewhere in a plastic bag:

1½ cups of sugar
2 tablespoons of cornstarch
½ teaspoon of cinnamon
¼ teaspoon of nutmeg (optional)

(This is the recommended amount for four cups of fresh berries, so use the mixture accordingly.)

The sugar-spice mix, berries and biscuit mix are the makings for a great tasting blueberry, raspberry, or strawberry cobbler. Just stir the berries and sugar-spice mix together in a dish, cover with biscuit dough, and bake in the reflector oven for 30 to 45 minutes.

Fancy Baking: If you have extra biscuit mix and some spare eggs (dried or fresh), you can put together some tasty scones:

Make up the biscuit dough as usual, but add an egg or two for richness, and maybe some raisins. Sprinkle the scones with a sugar-cinnamon mix, brown sugar, or even plain sugar before setting them to bake.

Fresh Fruit: If you plan to take along fresh fruit in your cooler, give the fruit the extra protection of a double-thick grocery bag. This will prevent spots on the fruit from freezing when they come in contact with the zero-degree ice and frozen food.

Stove Fuel: If you do your cooking on a gas stove, as I do, do not try to save money by using unleaded automobile gasoline. Any savings you might realize in fuel cost will be consumed in buying replacement generators, and you will have the frequent frustration of generators going bad just when you need them most. I burn 8 to 10 gallons of stove fuel per season. On the average I replace one generator per season; with improper fuel, I would need several.

3 For a Safe Journey

There is no way to over-emphasize the importance of being safety-conscious when in a wilderness situation. It is the inexperienced or thoughtless trip leader who is plagued with accidents, some very tense situations, and perhaps even a tragedy. Each season, we read in the papers of the effects of these careless leaders: numerous drownings and near-drownings are reported, along with other mishaps.

The average person reads of these tragedies and thinks, "Isn't that a shame," or "Isn't it lucky they were saved." Unless a relative or friend is involved, or they are somehow affected, the majority of readers do not give the accident another thought. Being professionally interested, I have looked a little deeper into some of these reports and, almost without exception, the root cause is inexperience or carelessness on the part of the leader, if there *was* a leader! "I didn't think the wind was that strong." "The rapids didn't look *that* bad." "I thought we could make it before dark." These are a few quotes from luckless leaders. Usually, they are young college students who have been put in charge of a group of teen-agers, their only qualification being, perhaps, that they had been on a canoe trip before.

I once asked a Boy Scout leader, whose troop was ready to run Chase Rapids on the Allagash River, how he'd prepared the boys for their white water run. "Oh," he said, "God looks after little boys in white water. We just turn them loose and regroup on the other end." This is not an isolated case, by any means.

Another time, I was camped at the foot of an unrunnable set of rapids. I saw a group come down the carry trail with a boy on a litter. I went to the first adult I saw to ask what had happened and to see whether I could help. He was so drunk he could only mumble, "We didn't know." The boys had gone ahead and started down the rapids; they upset, and the injury resulted. The other men in the group were in no better shape than the one I talked with, and I had to get the story from one of the boys. Fortunately, the injury was not serious enough to require evacuation of the victim.

Most states have no law requiring qualified trip leaders, or if they do, the law is so watered down that it is next to useless. It is imperative, then, that the conscientious person in charge put his or her own mind in gear and keep safety as a foremost consideration. Your judgment of your group's skills and abilities is often the deciding factor, but if in doubt, remember: No one ever drowned on a portage.

Preparation

Like all of the rest of the guide's responsibilities, that for group safety starts at home. He or she must consider what conditions *will* be met, what *might* be met, and what must be done to prepare for them.

As the conditions are considered, the equipment needed to meet them is made ready at home; thus, when the leader drives out of the yard, he or she knows that everything possible has been done in advance to ensure the safety and well-being of the party.

Canoes
Nearly everyone buying a first canoe gets one that is too small. Non-canoeists may be more familiar with boats and their lengths, and since a twelve-foot boat is a fairly large one, they'll reason that a fourteen- or sixteen-foot canoe should be more than adequate for any kind of water. They couldn't be more wrong! These little canoes

are designed for use in small protected ponds or streams where there is no chance of heavy wind, white water, or anything other than the occupants to effect the canoe. Anyone who takes one of these loaded out onto a large lake or in a white water river is flirting with danger. Of course, the experienced canoeist can do it and get away with it, but, then, few experienced canoeists would do it.

I furnish canoes for the trips I guide, and they are all *at least* eighteen feet long. My own is a twenty-footer because I carry a heavier load than my guests. I cannot think of any circumstances where the eighteen or twenty feet has been a disadvantage, but the advantages are not hard to recognize when you are underway.

The space available for storing gear is the first factor that becomes apparent when you start loading up. In the small canoe, the things that cannot fit on the bottom must be piled on top of something else. This raises the center of gravity, and the canoe becomes tippy. In the large canoe the gear can be spread out and kept low, making the canoe very stable. A properly loaded canoe is very hard to tip over; in fact, it is much more stable than when empty. It may ship water in heavy waves, but to actually tip it over would require conscious effort by the paddlers. (There are exceptions, like broaching against a rock in white water.)

Many people do not realize the difference an extra foot in the length of a canoe can make. Consider the difference between a sixteen-footer and a seventeen-footer: One foot, obviously. But, where in the canoe is that extra foot? Right in the middle! In the middle, where the canoe is the broadest and where the maximum buoyancy will be added. I think this justifies the leader in saying that a sixteen-footer is not adequate, while a seventeen-footer is okay. To the novice it may seem like nit-picking, but that extra foot is, literally, a big one.

Six inches of freeboard is the oft-quoted standard for a loaded canoe, and this is a good rule of thumb, but one should not lose sight of the fact that six inches is an adequate margin of safety for the *average canoe*. There are exceptions, as with any rule. For example, the very popular Old Town Tripper is a little over seventeen feet long and is *fifteen inches* deep at the center. This is three inches deeper than the average seventeen-foot canoe, and it means that if this canoe is loaded until the rail is within six inches of the water, there would be nine inches below water. This would be overloaded, in my opinion: The canoe would be sluggish and slow to respond to the paddle—a good recipe for trouble. However, few people find it necessary to load the Tripper that heavily, and it has become a

Canoes must be large enough to efficiently stow away gear.

favorite with guides and outfitters for rental purposes—a pretty good recommendation.

The very long, narrow racing-type canoes are seen now and then on a canoe trip. The suitability of these canoes for this purpose is questionable because they were designed not to carry a load, but rather to cut through the water with a minimum of resistance. People who own these canoes may not be experienced trippers, but they are usually experienced canoe handlers and therefore have a good idea of the limitations of their crafts. Racing canoes are definitely not recommended for the novice.

If your people are furnishing their own canoes, insist that they be at least seventeen feet long and of more or less standard construction. That is, avoid the cheapies made with about a ten-inch depth, even though they may be of adequate length. If possible, look the canoes over prior to the trip; don't take it for granted that your charges will have brought their canoes in the peak of condition. A little thing like missing seat bolt might not be disastrous, but would be a real annoyance on a week-long trip. How easily this can be fixed at home, but how difficult it is to find a bolt in the woods! An unexpected hole or rip could be repaired, but—what a sour note on which to start a canoe vacation.

I met the epitome of neglect on the Allagash one summer. An elderly man and his grandson were taking the one hundred mile trip with an eighteen-foot canoe and a small outboard motor. They came paddling into my camp looking for someone with tools they could use to work on the motor. My meager tools were not much help because the motor was frozen—it would not turn over. As we talked I learned that he had not even tried to turn the motor over since using it the previous fall! I was appalled by this, and could not help feeling sorry for this gentleman. I directed him to the nearest ranger who had a well-equipped tool box at his cabin. I learned later that they eventually got the motor going, but think how much trouble he could have avoided by simply trying the motor at home.

The material that the canoes are made of is not too important as long as they are well made. The argument of which is the best canoe material will go on and on, with each canoeist reaching his or her own conclusion.

My own stable of canoes includes a couple of eighteen-foot, shoe keel aluminum Grummans, and the rest are eighteen-and twenty-foot strip canoes—I built them myself, of cedar and fiberglass. The aluminum canoes, while they have their disadvantages, are tough! If some of my people have had no experience, they get the metal ones, while the more skilled get to use the hand-crafted wooden canoes.

I have to admit that using the strip canoes is not entirely practical for this purpose. They don't get the tender loving care that the owner of such a canoe would give it. I do get some deep scratches and a hole now and then, but these can be easily repaired, and this disadvantage is over-shadowed by the pleasure I get in seeing these canoes perform on the lakes and rivers. My guests appreciate them, too, and some vow to build one for themselves.

If I were going to be completely practical I would furnish either aluminum or ABS canoes for rental purposes. These will withstand the careless abuse that they might receive from a non-owner who is just learning to canoe.

The better the canoe handler, the less important is the choice of canoe or canoe material. A good many guides here in Maine still go up and down the rivers in their twenty-foot guide canoes built of cedar and canvas. How distinctly these stand out from a distance as they move along among the brightly colored ABS or aluminum canoes of the rest of the party!

Life Preservers—PFD's

On several occasions I have been caught out on a large lake in a sudden, unexpected wind—not an uncommon occurrence in mid-summer. As my guests and I put on our Personal Flotation Devices (PFD's), I have always thought to myself, "What a blessing these things are" a blessing especially to one who has the responsibility for several lives. The margin of safety these PFD's give when one is unexpectedly dunked is unbelievable unless it has been experienced. The colder the water, the greater the benefit, and the greater the believer in life preservers you become.

Personal Flotation Devices are made in five types and numbered with Roman numerals:

(1) Type I PFD
(2) Type II PFD
(3) Type III PFD
(4) Type IV PFD
(5) Type V PFD

These classifications are in the order of decreasing usefulness or desirability. That is, if you found yourself struggling in cold water, you would be far happier to be wearing a Type I PFD than to be hanging onto a Type IV. Only the first four are legal or suitable for canoeing; Types II and III are those most commonly used by canoe trippers and outdoor people.

Type I: This jacket-style PFD has the greatest amount of buoyancy, and is designed to turn an unconscious person to a slightly backward position and to maintain the position. The Type I would be the choice of white water rafters and kayakers challenging Class IV and V white water, and for wilderness canoe travelers who will run heavy white water, especially during cold weather periods.

Type II: This PFD will also turn most wearers to a slightly backward position, but its ability to do so is not as pronounced as with a Type I. This PFD is more comfortable than the Type I and is sized as follows: Adult (more than 90 pounds), Medium Child (50 to 90 pounds), Small Child (less than 50 pounds) and Small Child (less

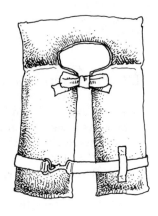

Type I PFD.   *Type II PFD.*

than 30 pounds). This is the PFD that is generally referred to as the "horsecollar" and is the least expensive and most commonly used device for summer canoe trips. It allows free use of arms and shoulders and so does not interfere with paddling or poling.

Type III: With this PFD the wearer must put himself or herself in the slightly backward position and then the device will maintain that position. The Type III comes in variety of sizes and styles to match body size and expected activity. For cool weather use, the Type III PFD is great. Either the vest or jacket style will keep the upper body warm while you are paddling, and in the event of an upset the insulation will trap body heat and help prevent hypothermia. In warm weather, though, this type of PFD is uncomfortably hot.

Type IV: The Type IV PFD is designed to be grasped and held onto until rescue. It is legal and is better than nothing, but it should *definitely not* be considered for wilderness canoe tripping.

Type V: This includes devices such as water ski belts; these are neither legal nor suitable for canoeing.

I furnish the Type II PFD's for my guests. They are inexpensive

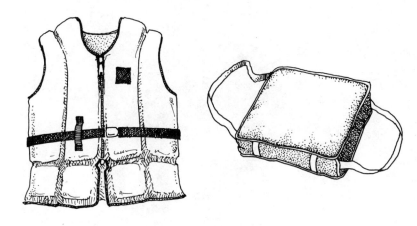

and offer good protection. I get about two or three years of good service from them before it is necessary to replace them. I *do not* allow people to use the PFD's as seat cushions or kneeling pads; I caution my guests that these things can save their lives, and ask that they treat them accordingly. The only unusual use I make of them is as shoulder pads for portaging a canoe, and for a pillow at night. The portaging is too infrequent to damage them, and the weight of a person's head is not enough to do any harm.

I have a Type III PFD myself, and I like it very much in the cool times of the year. However, during the hot weather I find it uncomfortable, and I use the horsecollar.

In preparation for a canoe trip all PFD's should be carefully checked for rips, tears, punctures and any other signs of wear that could make them unsuitable *and* unsafe for use. Make sure you have the correct size for everyone in the party. It is unsafe for a child to wear an adult size PFD. Bigger isn't better! If the people are furnishing their own PFD's be sure they are adequate and meet the Coast Guard regulations. Under no circumstances should a leader settle for a Type IV PFD. If someone's fanny is so tender that he/she needs a cushion, let the person bring a pillow, but keep the PFD's to the type that can be worn.

As I mentioned before, I furnish the Type II to my people for summertime use. I think that if I took a lot of cold weather trips, I

Properly fitted PFD's are a must for safe, care-free enjoyment of white water. Type II, "horsecollar," in the bow, Type III in the stern.

would provide or require the Type III for the extra warmth it gives both out of the water and, if it comes to it, in the water.

No item of equipment is more important for your guest's well-being and safety than their life preservers. You can have a lot of things go wrong on a trip and still rate it as a success, but if there is a death or serious injury that you could have prevented, *Man, you're a failure!*

Medical Preparation

I'm covering this in the preparation section because we all hope that this is where medical experience will rest, not to be called upon while underway. No one minds bringing home unused medical supplies, but the leader cannot afford to throw a few band-aids in his pack and call it sufficient preparation. Advanced knowledge of first aid and a complete kit of medical supplies are absolute musts!

I have avoided calling this section "First Aid" because First Aid is taught with the assumption that the patient can reach a doctor or hospital within 30 minutes or so. Of course, on a wilderness canoe trip this is not possible, and any treatment must be handled accordingly.

I do not list the contents of a wilderness medical kit because I feel a person should make up his or her own in accordance with his/her ability to use it. I do highly recommend the book *Wilderness Medicine* by William W. Forgey, M.D., Indiana Camp Supply Books, 405 Osborne, Pittsboro, Indiana 46167, 1979. In it you will find two lists of drugs and equipment, one prescription and one non-prescription. Another excellent, though a little older, book is *Being Your Own Wilderness Doctor* by Dr. E. Russel Kodet and Bradford Angier, Pocket Books, New York, 1974. Both books describe the symptoms and treatment for all of the things that we don't like to think about happening, but that we know can. Just scanning the headings is sobering, for you have to realize all the emergencies that might have to be faced.

Do your homework in the medical department. While we do not call wilderness medicine first aid, the courses offered in first aid are the most valuable training that a leader can get. It is imperative that *at least* a basic course be taken, and of further training the more the better. Most instructors of these courses are qualified and willing to give special advice and instruction if you make them aware of your special needs.

My own medical supplies are carried in two kits. The smaller kit is for the usual scrapes, cuts, and abrasions that make up 99 percent of the medical treatment needed on a canoe trip, and I keep it in my personal pack where it is always handy. When I have young teenagers along, I keep things even handier by filling one of my shirt pockets with a supply of band-aids. I can dispense a dozen or more band-aids per day; it is unbelievable, the number of those things a group of kids can use up in a week or so. Take plenty!

The larger medical kit contains the more serious supplies, and I keep it in the tool pack. This kit is seldom used, so I make a point of carefully checking it at least once per season to be sure everything is still serviceable, up to date, and undamaged. If I use something from the kit, I make note of it so that I'll not forget to replace it as soon as we return to civilization.

Part of your advance preparation for a trip is to become aware of any special medical problems of your guests. Be sure to ask them about this: know what the problem is and how to administer whatever treatment may be required. If that treatment must be given with an injection, then be sure you are capable of giving one.

It is not uncommon to have someone along who is allergic to bee stings. I have encountered this several times. In every case the person brought along the proper kit for treatment, but the responsibility for using that kit was mine. The treatment involves giving a shot; it isn't hard, but speed is important—there's no time to stop and read directions.

People who depend on glasses, particularly those who cannot see without them, should be reminded and urged to carry spares. Glasses are easily dropped overboard—lost forever. A glasses strap is an excellent precaution.

I can think of nothing so satisfying as helping a handicapped person to make a wilderness canoe trip. It is an experience such a person could never hope to have except in the company of a responsible, woods-wise guide. If you ever have such an opportunity, I highly recommend it—the adventure may well do you more good than it does the person you are responsible for!

I speak from experience. One member of a group of young people I guided on a river trip was legally blind. I got to know him quite well before the trip, and I was impressed with his positive attitude toward life and the future. He was realistic, and we openly discussed his problem and the trip we were going to undertake. I also talked with his mother, who, though worried, was anxious for him to have the experience.

The boy was bow paddler in my canoe, and a good one. He couldn't see the rocks when we ran white water, but he was well-coordinated and would respond instantly to my commands, drawing right or left without hesitation. We never touched a rock, and in our cooperation quite a camaraderie built up between us. As a group member he pulled his own weight, doing camp chores every bit as well as anyone else. There is no doubt in anyone's mind that he will pull his own weight through life, as well.

Each handicapped person must be considered according to his or her particular problems, but *do* consider taking someone on a wilderness trip if you have the opportunity. If the trip seems feasible for the person, then by all means do it. You'll never regret it!

The less you leave to chance in your safety preparations, the fewer chances you'll take. Enough things happen that cannot possibly be anticipated; don't make matters worse by ignoring the things that *can* be planned for.

Underway

When I was a small boy, the radio was to us what TV is to kids today. We each had programs we listened to regularly, and one of my favorites was a short one called *The Story Man.* Each weekday morning, he told a five-minute story and then signed off with a safety slogan: "Always alert, never get hurt." With these words ringing in my ears every morning, I kissed my mother goodbye and dashed out to catch the school bus.

"Always alert, never get hurt"—it must have been deeply etched in my brain as a boy growing up in rural Maine, because it still comes to mind forty-odd years later. It *is* good advice, and I try to follow it on my trips. The canoe guide has to be constantly alert to the hazards that may threaten the safety of his or her people—not only alert to the present, but with plans formulated to deal with dangers that will be faced later in the day or in the days to come.

If you decide ahead of time that your party cannot handle a Class III rapid that is coming up, then you *and* they will be prepared. They will know that they face a portage, and you will have the confidence that comes with pre-planning. For sure, you will have uncertainties about some situations, but you'll hash them out in your own mind ahead of time so that your attitude toward the guests is firm and confident. You'll tell them, "We cannot run this white water," not: "We might be able to make it, but maybe we'd better not."

The most common dangers that must be coped with are white water on the rivers and wind on flat water,especially when when crossing large lakes. Then, there is the threat of hypothermia in the colder times of the year and at all times in the northern areas. While these things are not all of the dangers that may threaten a canoe party, they are responsible for a large majority of canoeing accidents and so should be given plenty of thought by the trip leader. I strongly urge that you consider the dangerous circumstances that may arise and establish rules of thumb that will make on-the-spot decision-making easier. For example, these are some of my safety rules for the wearing of life jackets: (1) always wear them in the spring and fall when the water is cold; (2) wear them for all rapids above Class I; (3) wear them when there is anything more than a breeze on a large lake; (4) when in doubt, wear them. I have others for these and other situations and they *are* rules of thumb, not absolute. They can be changed and bent, but the interest of safety is foremost.

Wind

I think the danger of upset among inexperienced canoeists is as great on windy flat water with large waves as it is in white water with the rocks, standing waves, souse holes, and what have you. Canoe control is important in either situation, but the strong wind encountered on big lakes creates the added problem of power—the power that you need to keep the canoe progressing into the wind and at the same time maintain control. Most new paddlers have not canoed enough to develop the stamina needed for sustained paddling and control when facing a direct or quartering wind.

It is always a matter of judgment whether or not to move on a windy day. Only experience can teach this; you develop an eye and an ear for the wind. If the leader does deem it safe to move, he should not plan on covering too many miles. It is a discouraging thing for someone who is just learning to control a canoe to have to fight a wind while practicing canoe strokes. This can cause bad habits to develop—switch-paddling, for example. It would be much better, in your pre-trip planning, to allow for one or two wind-bound days when large lakes must be crossed. If you don't happen to get wind-bound, everyone will appreciate a lay-over of a day or two at a favored campsite later on. Usually, though, these extra days are hard to come by.

Some of my most-used canoe routes in Maine run north. The most common fair-weather wind direction is from the north or northwest. Therefore, I have spent many, many days on shore waiting for the wind to calm.

The most practical way to progress when days are windy is to travel early and late. If the wind blows, it usually blows the hardest in the middle of the day. Often we move after supper in the evening, and from daybreak until eight or nine in the morning.

If you expect wind and plan to move in the early morning, fix a snack the evening before that can be eaten while underway. Plan breakfast, or brunch, for when you get to your destination. Most groups can get up and underway in a half hour if breakfast is not served. We sometimes get in as much as three hours of calm paddling before the air starts to move again. Sometimes the wind decides not to blow that day after all, and we find ourselves with a lot of time on our hands for the rest of the day, but there are always ways to use it and no one complains.

Adjusting the daily routine to the whims of nature can be gratifying. I think this spirit of living *with* nature rather than fighting it is important and meaningful; it is a valuable lesson in living. The wind

Windbound! Canoeists sunbathe on the lee side of this island while the windward side is battered with 3-foot waves.

could be bucked with motors in most cases, but how much more satisfying it is to move with the elements instead of slugging it out with them!

As I mentioned, many of my trips move against prevailing winds. These winds are a constant frustration to me as I try to plan and replan our moves to finish the trip on schedule. Most people canoe during their vacations. Their vacations end at specific times of the week or month, so they don't have time for unexpected delays. If someone's vacation ends on the twelfth, he or she will more than likely want to be back at work on the thirteenth. To date I have never missed a take-out time, but some of my gray hairs are from figuring how to do it. I wouldn't endanger any of my guests' lives, even if it meant they would be a week late for work, but it is part of the challenge to get them there safely and on time. As I look back on various trips, remembering times when there seemed to be no way to progress to the take-out point on time, the frustration of the moment is a source of pride. Somehow, we've always managed to make it.

For a Safe Journey 55

Wind can be a threat when you're off the water as well as when you're afloat on it. Be sure that tents are pitched in a sheltered area, with no danger of falling trees or limbs. Check on this *before* the tents are pitched; people don't enjoy putting up and taking down tents, so expect to be unpopular for awhile if you must give them some extra practice. Most people just select the smoothest, softest spot without regard for anything else. Help them out first, and get your own tent up later.

While you are ashore, the canoes should be secure and placed in a sheltered spot. This may seem an obvious point, but peculiar things can happen to the unwary. I was sitting out a blow on Eagle Lake one day when I looked up and saw a seventeen-foot aluminum canoe fly by! Some people nearby had left their canoe upside down on the rocky beach. The wind carried it at least a hundred feet before letting it down. Fortunately, it landed in the water and there was no damage. Carry the canoes into the woods, or tie them down securely if there is no shelter.

One final thought on lake canoeing and the wind: I think most people get into trouble on windy lakes because they learned their high school geometry too well. "The shortest distance between two points is a straight line," they reason, and instead of following the longer, yet safer, shoreline they head out across the biggest part of the lake to cut down on mileage. This is often a mistake for two reasons.

The first reason is obvious: the safety of a nearby shore in case of an accidental dunking. Also, the wind will surely be diminished by nearby land and trees.

The second reason does not concern safety but is important, nevertheless. Paddling in the middle of a large lake is downright boring. Distant shorelines are of little or no interest, and progress is difficult to perceive without the apparent movement of nearby fixed objects on land. I don't mean you have to paddle into every little cove, adding miles and miles to the trip, but try to follow a course that jumps from point to point along the shore. I find that much of my lake paddling can be done from 100 yards offshore to within a paddle's length of it. If I add a mile or two to the day's travel, so what? They will be enjoyable miles, and that's what we're there for.

So, use the shoreline. It is safer and far more interesting. The difference in interest is the same as that of driving down a freeway or driving down a country lane. One is a lot faster, but the other is much more appealing.

White Water

The potential danger to people and equipment in white water depends on the class of white water you encounter and the experience of the people involved. If rivers were made to order for trip leaders, they would start out with a nice easy Class I current to train people on, then progress through Class II and on to a nice Class III to wind up the trip with a grand finale.

Few rivers meet these criteria, and so we make do with what each one offers, and compromise. But, don't compromise with safety. Caution people about the dangers that exist even in mild current. When you tell them what to do in case they broach against a rock, explain why the most natural reaction for novices is to lean upstream to counteract the impact. This should be avoided, of course, but *stress it* so that they will think about it and realize why they must lean downstream. When you explain the action of the

They forgot to lean downstream! Both *were wearing PFD's at the time of the mishap.*

water rolling the canoe until the gunwale dips under and the canoe fills up, it becomes clear and helps them when they must react instantly.

One good way to illustrate the power of even a mild current is to find an excuse for them to paddle upstream for a while. They'll believe!

Caution your novices against getting downstream of their canoe if they should find themselves in the water—the filled canoe could pin and even crush someone against a rock. There is little chance of injury if they position themselves with their feet downstream to fend off rocks, and just ride it out to quiet water below. With the security of the life preserver holding them up, most people even enjoy the experience.

Try to keep the group close together so that you are nearby to assist if someone gets into trouble. This isn't always easy, but all you can do is try. This brings up a question about where the guide should be positioned: In front? In the middle? At the end? Of course, if you have an assistant with experience similar to yours, then the solution is easy—one in front and one in the rear. I make part of my living guiding, and I cannot afford this luxury. I always lead the group. There is room for criticism of this position, and I recognize it. However, I have found that my guests feel most confident with me showing the easiest channel and looking for trouble ahead.

The biggest disadvantage of taking the lead is that if any of my guests capsize, I am downstream from them and thus in a difficult position to render immediate assistance. I compensate by trying to keep all canoes as close together as is practical and still have room to maneuver. This is not always easy, and I think this question is a matter of personal choice. I repeat, though: the guests prefer the leader out in front. Remember, everything is unfamiliar to them. You know what is coming up, or can at least recognize potential dangers. People fear the unknown, and what's around the next bend of the river is unknown to them.

The American Whitewater Affiliation has published a safety code that should be read and re-read by persons taking parties on white water canoe trips. The code is written to include canoes, kayaks and rafts, and the purpose is to make white water caonoeing as safe as it is enjoyable. The following is the AWA code in its entirety:

Safety Code

Personal Preparedness and Responsibility

1. **Be a Competent Swimmer** with ability to handle yourself underwater.
2. **Wear** a Lifejacket.
3. **Keep Your Craft Under Control.** Control must be good enough at all times to stop or reach shore before you reach any danger. Do not enter a rapid unless you are reasonably sure you can safely navigate it or swim the entire rapid in event of capsize.
4. **Be Aware of River Hazards and Avoid Them.** Following are the most frequent **killers.**
   A. **High Water**: The river's power and danger, and the difficulty of rescue increase tremendously as the flow rate increases. It is often misleading to judge river level at the put-in. Look at a narrow, critical passage. Could a *sudden* rise from sun on a snow pack, rain, or a dam release occur on your trip?
   B. **Cold**: Cold quickly robs one's strength, along with one's will and ability to save oneself. Dress to protect yourself from cold water and weather extremes. When the water temperature is less than 50 degrees F., a diver's wetsuit is essential for safety in event of an upset. Next best is wool clothing under a windproof outer garment such as a splash-proof nylon shell; in this case one should also carry matches and a complete change of clothes in a waterproof package. If, after prolonged exposure, a person experiences uncontrollable shaking or has difficulty talking and moving, he must be warmed immediately by whatever means available.
   C. **Strainers**: Brush, fallen trees, bridge pilings, or anything else which allows river current to sweep through but pins boat and boater against the obstacle. The water pressure on anything trapped this way is overwhelming, and there may be little or no whitewater to warn of danger.
   D. **Weirs, Reversals, and Souse Holes**: The water drops over an obstacle, then curls back on itself in a stationary wave, as is often seen at weirs and dams. The surface water is actually going **upstream**, and this action will trap any floating object between the drop and the wave. Once trapped, a swimmer's only hope is to dive below the surface where the current is flowing downstream, or try to swim out the end of the wave.

5. **Boating Alone** is not recommended. The preferred minimum is three craft.
6. **Have a Frank Knowledge of Your Boating Ability.** Don't attempt waters beyond this ability. Learn paddling skills and teamwork, if in a multiple-manned craft, to match the river you plan to boat.
7. **Be in Good Physical Condition** consistent with the difficulties that may be expected.
8. **Be Practiced in Escape** from an overturned craft, in self rescue, in rescue and in **Artificial Respiration.** Know first aid.
9. **The Eskimo Roll** should be mastered by kayakers and canoeists planning to run large rivers and/or rivers with continuous rapids where a swimmer would have trouble reaching shore.
10. **Wear a Crash Helmet** where an upset is likely. This is essential in a kayak or covered canoe.
11. **Be Suitably Equipped.** Wear shoes that will protect your feet during a bad swim or a walk for help, yet will not interfere with swimming (tennis shoes recommended). Carry a knife and waterproof matches. If you need eyeglasses, tie them on and carry a spare pair. Do not wear bulky clothing that will interfere with your swimming when water-logged.

Boat and Equipment Preparedness

1. **Test New and Unfamiliar Equipment** before relying on it for difficult runs.
2. **Be Sure Craft is in Good Repair** before starting a trip. Eliminate sharp projections that could cause injury during a swim.
3. Inflatable craft should have **Multiple Air Chambers** and should be test inflated before starting a trip.
4. **Have Strong, Adequately Sized Paddles or Oars** for controlling the craft and carry sufficient spares for the length of the trip.
5. **Install Flotation Devices** in non-inflatable craft, securely fixed, and designed to displace as much water from the craft as possible.
6. **Be Certain There is Absolutely Nothing to Cause Entanglement** when coming free from an upset craft; i.e., a spray skirt that won't release or tangles around legs; life jacket buckles or clothing that might snag; canoe seats that lock on shoe heels; foot braces that fail or allow feet to jam under them; flexible decks that collapse on boater's legs when a kayak is trapped by water pressure; baggage that dangles in an upset; loose rope in the craft, or badly secured bow/stern lines.

7. **Provide Ropes to Allow You to Hold Onto Your Craft** in case of upset, and so that it may be rescued. Following are the recommended methods:

  A. **Kayaks and Covered Canoes** should have 6 inch diameter grab loops of ¼ inch rope attached to bow and stern. A stern painter 7 or 8 feet long is optional and may be used if properly secured to prevent entanglement.

  B. **Open Canoes** should have bow and stern lines (painters) securely attached consisting of 8 to 10 feet of ¼ or ⅜ inch rope. These lines must be *secured* in such a way that they will not come loose accidentally and entangle the boaters during a swim, yet they must be ready for immediate use during an emergency. Attached balls, floats, and knots are *not* recommended.

  C. **Rafts and Dories** should have taut perimeter grab lines threaded through the loops usually provided.

8. **Respect Rules for Craft Capacity** and know how these capacities should be reduced for whitewater use. (Life raft ratings must generally be halved.)

9. **Carry Appropriate Repair Materials:** tape (heating duct tape) for short trips, complete repair kit for wilderness trips.

10. **Car Top Racks Must Be Strong** and positively attached to the vehicle, and each boat must be tied to each rack. In addition, each end of each boat should be tied to car bumper. Suction cup racks are poor. The entire arrangement should be able to withstand all but the most violent vehicle accident.

Leader's Preparedness and Responsibility

1. **River Conditions:** Have a reasonable knowledge of the difficult parts of the run, or if an exploratory trip, examine maps to estimate the feasibility of the run. Be aware of possible rapid changes in river level, and how these changes can affect the difficulty of the run. If important, determine approximate flow rate or level. If trip involves important tidal currents, secure tide information.

2. **Participants:** Inform participants of expected river conditions and determine if the prospective boaters are qualified for the trip. All decisions should be based on group safety and comfort. Difficult decisions on the participation of marginal boaters must be based on total group strength.

3. **Equipment:** Plan so that all necessary group equipment is present on the trip; 50 to 100 foot throwing rope, first aid kit with fresh

and adequate supplies, extra paddles, repair materials, and survival equipment if appropriate. Check equipment as necessary at the put-in, especially: life jackets, boat flotation, and any items that could prevent complete escape from the boat in case of an upset.

4. **Organization**: Remind each member of individual responsibility in keeping group compact and intact between leader and sweep (capable rear boater). If group is too large, divide into smaller groups, each of appropriate boating strength, and designate group leaders and sweeps.

5. **Float Plan:** If trip is into a wilderness area, or for an extended period, your plans should be filed with appropriate authorities, or left with someone who will contact them after a certain time. Establishment of checkpoints along the way at which civilization could be contacted if necessary should be considered. Knowing location of possible help could speed rescue in any case.

In Case of Upset

1. **Evacuate Your Boat Immediately** if there is imminent danger of being trapped against logs, brush, or any other form of strainer.

2. **Recover With an Eskimo Roll if Possible.**

3. **If You Swim, Hold Onto Your Craft**. It has much flotation and is easy for rescuers to spot. Get to the upstream end so craft cannot crush you against obstacles.

4. **Release Your Craft if This Improves Your Safety.** If rescue is not imminent and water is numbing cold, or if worse rapids follow, then strike out for the nearest shore.

5. **When Swimming Rocky Rapids,** use backstroke with legs downstream and **Feet Near the Surface**. If your foot wedges on the bottom, fast water will push you under and hold you there. **Get to Slow or Very Shallow Water Before Trying to Stand or Walk. Look Ahead.** Avoid possible entrapment situations: rock wedges, fissures, strainers, brush, logs, weirs, reversals and souse holes. Watch for eddies and slack-water so that you can be ready to use these when you approach. Use every opportunity to work your way toward shore.

6. If others spill, **Go After the Boaters**. Rescue boats and equipment only if this can be done safely.

International Scale of River Difficulty

(If rapids on a river generally fit into one of the following classifications, but the water temperature is below 50 degrees F., or if the trip is an extended trip in a wilderness area, the river should be considered one class more difficult than normal.)

Class I: Moving water with a few riffles and small waves. Few or no obstructions.

Class II: Easy rapids with waves up to 3 feet, and wide, clear channels that are obvious without scouting. Some maneuvering is required.

Class III: Rapids with high, irregular waves often capable of swamping an open canoe. Narrow passages that often require complex maneuvering. May require scouting from shore.

Class IV: Long, difficult rapids with constricted passages that often require precise maneuvering in very turbulent waters. Scouting from shore is often necessary, and conditions make rescue difficult. Generally not possible for open canoes. Boaters in covered canoes and kayaks should be able to Eskimo roll.

Class V: Extremely difficult, long, and very violent rapids with highly congested routes which nearly always must be scouted from shore. Rescue conditions are difficult and there is significant hazard to life in event of a mishap. Ability to Eskimo roll is essential for kayaks and canoes.

Class VI: Difficulties of Class V carried to the extreme of navigability. Nearly impossible and very dangerous. For teams of experts only, after close study and with all precautions taken.

AMERICAN WHITEWATER AFFILIATION

A New System of Universal River Signals

Stop: Potential hazard ahead. Wait for "all clear" signal before proceeding, or scout ahead. Form a horizontal bar with your paddle or outstretched arms. Move up and down to attract attention, using a pumping motion with paddle or flying motion with arms. Those seeing the signal should pass it back to others in the party.

Help/Emergency: Assist the signaller as quickly as possible. Give three long blasts on a police whistle while waving a paddle, helmet or life vest over your head in a circular motion. If a whistle is not available, use the visual signal alone. A whistle is best carried on a lanyard attached to the shoulder of a life vest.

All Clear: Come ahead. (In the absence of other directions, proceed down the center.) Form a vertical bar with your paddle or one arm held high above your head. Paddle blade should be turned flat for maximum visibility. To signal direction or a preferred course through a rapid around obstruction, lower the previously vertical "all clear" by 45 degrees toward the side of the river with the preferred route. Never point toward the obstacle you wish to avoid.

Illustrations by Les Fry for AWA

Copies of this code may be obtained from: American Whitewater Affiliation, Safety Codes, P.O. Box 126, Jefferson City, Mo. 65102. If you would like to join this all-volunteer organization, contact Phil Vogel, Box 1483, Hagerstown, Md. 21704. Along with membership you will receive *American Whitewater*, a bi-monthly journal that is just great.

The white water runs are the high points of a wilderness canoe trip. They are exciting, but the guide must ensure that the people are ready for them and can make the descents safely. There are many good white water canoeing books on the market for beginners. One is *A White Water Handbook for Canoe and Kayak* by John T. Urban. It is published by, and available from, the Appalachian Mountain Club, 5 Joy St., Boston, Mass. 02108. Stick a copy in your pack before leaving home and leave it around where people can pick it up after they've tasted a little white water. Most are enthusiastic about reading and discussing the sport after they have experienced the thrill of a first run.

Hypothermia

It used to be called simply "exposure." Forget the semantics— people died from exposure, and they die from hypothermia. What this means is a lowered body temperature, and that can mean trouble when there is no warm, centrally heated house to retreat into at the first sign of a shiver or chill.

Our internal organs are designed to function at 98.6 degrees Farenheit. Any variation in this temperature can cause trouble. A difference of as little as ½ degree can cause illness—fever or chills. A difference of 5 degrees is a threat to life itself. The only good thing about this situation, at least for out-door people, is that the body is more tolerant of lower temperatures than higher ones.

When, due to exhaustion and overexposure to cold and wet, body heat is lost faster than it is produced, the body responds by making involuntary adjustments to preserve the normal temperature of internal organs. This results in a reduced blood flow to the extremities, and exercise is needed for the person to stay warm. In these circumstances the person often loses clarity of judgment, as well, which just makes matters worse.

The leader should learn to spot hypothermia in its early stages so that immediate steps can be taken. The following symptoms should not be ignored:

* Uncontrollable shivering
* Slurred speech, slow speech, vagueness
* Lapse in memory
* Immobility, fumbling
* Stumbling and lurching
* Drowsiness
* Exhaustion

The conditon of a hypothermia victim as listed here according to body temperature will give some idea of just how serious this thing can be:

98.6 - 91 degrees: Shivering becomes intense, difficult tasks are hard to perform.

91 - 86 degrees: Shivering decreases, muscle rigidity sets in. Poor muscle coordination and total amnesia may be present.

86 - 81 degrees: The victim becomes irrational and drifts into a stupor. Pulse and respiration decrease. At this point, an external heat source is more important than before, as the body has stopped producing heat. There is severe chance of cardiac arrest.

81 - 78 degrees: Heart becomes erratic. Most reflexes cease to function. The victim becomes unconcious.

Below 78 degrees: Cardiac and respiratory arrest occur, causing death.

Prevent hypothermia by being prepared for it. It is most commonly caused by a combination of cool or cold weather, water and exhaustion. Be sure everyone has good rain gear and warm clothes. Wool is preferred because it will insulate even when wet. Make a point of stressing this to your party. A lot of people think down filled clothing is the last word for outdoor wear. It isn't.

If the trip is in the spring or fall when water temperatures are extremely low, consider wearing wet suits, at least for the white water runs. A few minutes of immersion in 40-degree water could cause as much heat loss as a whole day of paddling in wet clothes. Anyone who has had even the briefest dunking in icy water should be closely watched for symptoms of hypothermia. Remember, too, that a victim may have already reached the first stages of hypothermia if an upset occurred in warmer water on a cold, wet day.

Don't be afraid of quitting somewhere short of the day's destination. If people start to get tired on a cold, damp day, you are asking for trouble if you push them. Don't forget that even camping in such weather conditions is far from ideal. Do everything possible to ensure people of a good, comfortable night's sleep.

Keep a supply of high energy snacks available for those cold wet days—candy, nuts, raisins, etc., can be just the fuel that the old furnace needs to keep producing life-giving heat. Make up a large batch of hot chocolate for folks to sip. It supplies heat and energy at the same time.

If it becomes necessary to treat someone for hypothermia, start by getting him or her out of the wet clothes and into some dry ones, into a dry sleeping bag, or both. Give the person warm, sweet liquids to drink and supply an external heat source. This source could be a warm fire, warm rocks placed around the sleeping bag, or another person, a heat donor, inside the bag with the victim. Both naked is best.

If you think that a party member has a case of advanced hypo-thermia, do everything in the previous paragraph, and then start determining how to evacuate the victim to a doctor or medical facility.

Don't ignore yourself in your concern for your party. One of the symptoms is impaired judgment! It is as important for their welfare that you take care of yourself as it is for you to care for them. Speed is especially essential when you suspect you yourself might be approaching hypothermia; quick action allows you to correct the problem before it reaches a more advanced stage, possibly endan-gering you and everyone else.

It would be impossible to anticipate everything that *could* go wrong for someone shepherding a group of inexperienced people through the wilderness. The first and greatest concern of the leader must be the safety of his or her guests. Good old common sense should prevail in situations involving safety, as it should in other aspects of canoe tripping. While we cannot overlook any potential danger to our people, neither can we be over-protective. At some point in time we must let them try out their own wings. You will be able to feel it when that time is right.

4 Canoe Power

"Locomotion: The act or power of moving from place to place."
One of the great things about canoe trips is the variety in methods
of locomotion. You don't just sit there paddling along in the canoe
day after day—each trip includes flat water paddling, white water
paddling, and some lazy days when you can drift along, letting the
current do most of the work. And if that is not enough variety,
there are portages. Sometimes, after several days on the water, I
actually find myself looking forward to a portage. It kind of breaks
things up and makes one appreciate all the more the easy-going life
in the canoe.

When the situation requires it, the setting pole can be unlimbered
and the canoeist can drive his or her craft against the current and
move upstream with surprising speed. Or, when there is barely
enough water to float the canoe, the pole allows the traveler to
negotiate downstream with ease.

The canoe can even be motorized and, while this use may be
controversial in some circles, it *does* add to the options and makes the
canoe an even more versatile craft.

Variety! Two days are never the same—neither the scenery nor the means of locomotion. It keeps things interesting and people happy.

Paddling Instructions

Sometimes I am fortunate enough to have people in my parties who are experienced canoeists, and the paddle is no stranger to their hands. However, this is not usually the case, and more often than not I find myself in the role of paddling instructor right from the first day on. Most have at least tried padding before, but I *have* had people who had never been in a canoe before the day we put in at the beginning of the trip.

The Allagash Wilderness Waterway offers some good news and some bad news to the novice paddler. The good news is that there are several days of quiet lake paddling to practice on before the rapidly flowing river is reached. The bad news is that Chase Rapids, the hardest to be encountered, makes up the first nine miles of travel on the river.

Now, Chase Rapids isn't the wild, churning, canoe-eating stretch of white water that some writers make it out to be, but it *does* have some Class III drops, and it *is* a challenge to an experienced paddler. To the uninitiated it can be downright intimidating. I use the days of lake travel to prepare my guests for the rapids ahead.

Paddling instruction is kept just as basic as possible, and the number of paddle strokes to learn kept to a minimum. First, they have to learn to keep the canoe running straight in quiet water without zig-zagging *and* without switching sides with their paddle every two or three strokes. I do this by demonstrating the "J" stroke and then paddling along ahead of them as we progress through the lakes. They can emulate my technique, and, at first, we go quite slowly to allow them to experiment and make mistakes without my looking on. I think this makes them more relaxed and less self-conscious as they struggle to grasp the fundamentals.

I always strongly recommend that my novices retain the same position in the canoe and the same partner for the entire trip. By doing this they have the opportunity to learn one position well, and to learn to work in coordination with a familiar partner. Versatility can be learned later.

I have always felt that a stern paddler can best learn canoe control by paddling solo. So, I encourage these people to take a canoe out

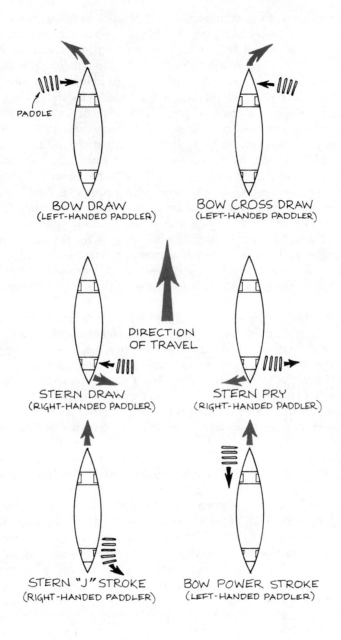

Basic strokes to get novices started downriver.

alone in the evening after supper and practice paddling *on one side* without switching. Once they are able to keep the canoe running straight alone, it will be a cinch with a bow paddler aboard. For many, these evening sessions lead to a lifetime addiction to solo canoeing as they discover the sheer joy of paddling slowly along a wilderness lake shore or through a quiet marsh by themselves.

None of the paddle strokes I teach first are difficult; in fact, they come naturally to anyone who spends enough time in a canoe. I remember how surprised I was years ago when I found that some things I had learned by myself to do with a paddle actually had a name and other people did them, too. Time is the secret: the people must spend as much time as possible with a paddle in their hands. After a while they will find themselves able to move the canoe where they want, and reacting without conscious thought to what they are doing. In the meantime, while waiting for the experience that comes with practice, it helps if they get some basics; and so, to teach paddle strokes, we have to name them. The drawing shows all of the strokes needed to get novice canoeists through a white water trip.

Their self-confidence soars as they discover that their canoe will move sideways, pivot, and turn in its own length with only these simple paddle strokes—the draws and the pry, along with the regular power stroke. I knew one paddler had "arrived" when he said, "You know, the 'J' stroke is nothing but a power stroke with a little pry on the end of it." That's it! There really are no white water strokes and flat water strokes; they are all just ways to make the canoe go where we want it to go, no matter what kind of water it is in.

Along with this small repertoire of paddle strokes, I introduce a similarly small lesson in river hydraulics. I tell them to avoid the vees that point (like arrows) upstream and to aim for the ones that point downstream. I explain that the upstream-pointing vee is caused by a rock at or near the surface, and the downstream-pointing vee is usually caused by deeper water flowing between two obstacles. With these two basics of river reading they can stay out of trouble, and through interest and observation can gain more knowledge as they go along. The longer the trip, the more time I have to teach new things.

The trip leader as a teacher will find that not all his or her pupils are eager to learn. This is frustrating, as any teacher knows, and one can't help but wonder why they are there in the first place. I'm afraid I don't have a magic solution for this situation. All the leader can do is try his or her best (and hope for the best). When there are people who refuse to try and will not take instruction, the leader is certainly justified in making these people portage any rapids that could cause injury or damage the canoe or equipment. This unfortunate situation is bound to cause hard feelings, but the leader must think of the overall welfare of the group as well as the personal safety of the people involved. A smashed canoe, lost gear, and injuries affect everyone in the party.

I was faced with a difficult decision on the Allagash with a group of six men. Actually, the decision was not difficult, but telling them of it was. As we progressed through the lakes it became evident to me that they were not going to learn the basic control strokes— they just would not try. As we approached Chase Rapids, I was sure they could not make the run, though by the way they talked I knew they expected to do so. I had to tell them they could not, but what made it even harder for them to swallow was the fact that my 11-year-old daughter, who was along as my bow partner, was capable of running the rapids and I was determined that she should.

They were disappointed and unhappy with me, but I knew in my own mind that I was right. My daughter was experienced in white water, and I had been drilling her in the different strokes as we paddled through the lakes. Still, I couldn't help feeling uncomfortable about my decision. A few days later one of their canoes upset in a much lesser rapid further down the river. There was no damage and everything was saved, but that evening one of them brightened up my day when he came up to me and told me that he now knew I had made the right decision back at Chase Rapids.

I mentioned earlier that I felt it was important to keep partners together throughout the trip. This is true as long as the partners are compatible, but don't lock your people into teams until you know you have the best combinations possible. Two strong paddlers in one canoe and two weak ones in another will just tend to string the group out. Not only that, but the weak ones will be trying so hard to keep up that they won't have time to learn proper canoe control and paddling technique.

It is much better that the strong paddlers be paired up with the weaker ones. If this is done diplomatically, no one's feelings need be hurt and everyone benefits. Of course, common sense should prevail. If you have husband and wife teams, then it would be unwise to suggest they start swapping around.

It is important that bow paddlers understand the importance of their position. In lake travel, the bow person is apt to feel that he or she is like just the work horse, while the stern person is responsible for all the canoe control. Make your bow paddlers realize that in white water is where they come into their own; that it is their quick decisions and reactions that keep the canoe off the rocks. This is true—with a good bow paddler, the stern person just follows through, keeping the canoe parallel with the current and enjoying the ride.

There is a lot more to handling a canoe than the simple techniques I have suggested in this chapter, as anyone in the position of trip leader already knows. But, things have to be taken one step at a time, and I'm a firm believer in the saying, "Success breeds success." If you can give your people the basic knowledge they need to successfully handle their canoes in flat water and white water, then their own enthusiasm will make them hungry for more and more

This was their first "taste" of white water. They had four days of flat-water paddling to practice basic strokes. Note the nice cross draw.

knowledge and skill. These you can give them if time permits, but if not, they will seek it out for themselves, anyway. You will have the satisfaction of knowing that you started them off on the right foot.

It is a satisfying thing for a guide to watch people with no previous experience handle their canoes with confidence. That smile they flash as they come bouncing through the standing waves is all the thanks that is needed.

Portaging

Sometime, ages ago, the birch bark canoe was invented by Stone Age man—the Indians of North America. There were many qualities that made this unique craft ideally suited to the needs of these early people, but one of the most important was its light weight. Its lightness meant portability. It was easily and quickly carried between watersheds, around rapids and over obstacles, and by one person!

Modern canoes, descendants of the Indian's canoe, still have the lightweight portability, but a lot of canoeists avoid waters with portages. This is a shame—they are missing out on some of the best and least used canoeing waters that we have. Novice canoeists have come to dread and thus avoid portages because they believe the stories told about them. It is human nature to exaggerate any difficult experience and make it sound even more difficult. If someone's difficult experience has found its way into print, then the description becomes even more believable.

One of the most famous and most written about portages in Maine is Mud Pond Carry. (The word *carry* is more often used in Maine than *portage*.) The carry is centuries old—it was used by Indians in their annual migration between coast and interior. One of the earliest mentions of it was by Henry David Thoreau in *The Maine Woods*, and he describes in detail the difficult trail, the insects, and everything else that would make any reasonable person think twice before attempting it. Actually, Thoreau had only to get his own body and personal pack across the two miles of land—his Indian guide did the rest of the work—but Thoreau didn't even accomplish this without getting lost. How he managed it is beyond me. Mud Pond Carry is a foot path that today is worn two feet deep in some places through centuries of use and erosion. I cannot believe it was too much different in the 1800's when he was there. Yet, he and his companion were lost for the better part of a day. At least this proved his wisdom in hiring an Indian guide—he should have stayed with him. Thoreau wrote:

> The Indian was greatly surprised that we should have taken what he called a 'tow' (i.e., tote or toting or supply) road instead of a carry path,—that we had not followed his tracks—said it was 'strange,' and evidently thought little of our woodcraft.

After reading Thoreau's account of Mud Pond Carry, I would dearly love to read a version of the same episode by their guide, Joe Polis. I have the mental picture of that poor guide hurrying around the woods trying to keep track of his charges while they wandered here and there gathering botanical samples and taking notes on the bird life they were observing.

My most memorable experience on Mud Pond Carry was with a group of young people—none over age fourteen, the youngest eleven. I was not looking foreward to the carry because I knew the youngsters were going to have difficulty managing canoes and equipment over the two miles. They were apprehensive about it too, having heard bits and pieces about the "terrible portage." I tried to maintain a cheerful and positive attitude about it, even though I had my doubts about their ability to move what looked to be a mountain of gear to Mud Pond. I kept asking myself what in the world I was doing taking these kids over such a difficult route.

We arrived at Umbazooksus Lake, the beginning of the carry, in mid-afternoon. I had not planned it that way, but the timing could not have been better, and I have planned it this way many times since. We had time to set up camp on the Umbazooksus end, and still carry our canoes to the mud Pond end before supper. Thus, we broke the difficult carry into two days.

I instructed the kids in how to make a two-person carry, with one at each end of the canoe and the forward edges of the seats resting on padded necks. They tried it, and after a bit of struggling and yelling at one another they guessed they could give it a try. I rigged my own canoe for a one-person carry and headed out for Mud Pond.

On my way back to Umbazooksus, I was surprised and pleased to see the progress the kids had made. Oh, they were griping and grumbling and allowed as how they doubted if they could make another 100 yards, but they trudged determinedly on toward Mud Pond. Except for one pair, who were the youngest and smallest, these kids got their canoes across the carry, and, the following day, all the gear that was in them. I helped the two little ones with their canoe, but they made up for it by making an extra trip for gear. Other than this, I carried nothing more than I would have had the party been all adults.

The mental preparedness of a group for a difficult portage is more important than their physical condition. Three or four or five canoes with all of the gear looks like an impossible amount of stuff to carry for any distance. The leader must make them realize that each individual does not carry *all* of that gear, but instead only *half* of what is in *one* canoe. When they look at it this way, the load seems a lot more manageable, and attitudes start to change. Don't get discouraged about the griping and growling that you'll hear. This goes with the territory, and while at the time they may wonder about your wisdom in leading them there, in the end they will take pride in what they have accomplished. So will you!

Preparing my canoe for portage.

The One-Person Carry

There are a number of ways of moving canoes across dry land. The best way, providing the person has the physical strength *and* self confidence, is the one-person carry. The paddles are spaced and tied in place so that they protrude just forward of the center thwart. Lacking a center thwart, it is necessary to span the distance between two thwarts with the paddles, and then the load is carried on the paddle shafts rather than on the flat of the blades. In either case, the shoulders should be padded. The best pads you are likely to have along are the "horsecollar"-style life preservers. With the "collar" resting further down on the back, the two upper straps are tied together behind the neck. The lower strap goes around the upper chest. This raises the two large pads from their usual position on the chest up to the shoulders.

The canoe can be hoisted onto the shoulders by the carrier alone, but this maneuver requires practice, especially with a large canoe, and is really not necessary because the canoe partner is standing there watching with nothing to do. It is much better that he or she hold up the bow while the carrier carefully gets into position and arranges the shoulder padding under the paddles. When ready, he or she stands up and walks off with the canoe, gripping the

Canoe portage pads made from a type II PFD.

A 20-foot guide canoe is easily carried over rough terrain by one person. Two people would be constantly working against one another.

gunwales, leaving the partner to start moving the gear.

The most important advantage of the one-person carry is that the person travels at his or her own pace, does not have to coordinate movements with a partner, and when tired, can rest the bow on a convenient limb without lowering the canoe to the ground. The disadvantage is that one person bears the weight of the canoe and must maneuver the bulk alone. A determined person will quickly develop the technique. My own twenty-foot guide canoe weighs about 100 pounds, but because the weight bears straight down on the shoulders it is relatively easy to carry. That same weight would be a very difficult load if it hung on the back like a backpack.

The Two-Person Carry
The two-person carry can be done in two ways. The first is for the

partners to place the forward edges of the seats on their necks (padded as I have already described). The hands are free to lift the canoe from time to time to relieve the pressure on the neck. By the second method, each person rests his/her end of the canoe on one shoulder, with one person on one side of the canoe and one on the other, with the canoe right side up. This method allows better visibility for the carriers, but requires stronger people.

No matter how much instruction you give in proper canoe carrying methods, some people will come up with their own unique, improbable, impractical method. No amount of urging a cajoling or arguing on your part will change their minds. This used to bother me as I watched them struggle, but no more. I figure that if I have showed them a couple of easy and acceptable ways of doing it and they still insist on doing it their way, then let them suffer. As long as they get the canoe to the other side in one piece and no one gets hurt, I'm happy.

Group Portages

Many times a portage consists of moving only 100 yards or so before the canoe's natural element is again reached. This might be to bypass a dam, an unrunnable falls, or some other obstacle. In this situation, if the terrain permits, I often line up six people (three on each side of the canoe) to carry each canoe, gear and all, to the put-in point. This saves a lot of unpacking and re-packing, and most people prefer to do it this way. I say "if terrain permits" because if you must move over a narrow trail or over very rough ground, this method causes some headaches, not to mention bruised shins, knees, and knuckles. It is almost impossible to coordinate six people with a heavy load around and between trees or down over ledges and boulders. Drop a loaded canoe on a rock, and you've got trouble!

Sometimes I use the same technique but lighten the load by removing part of the gear. This makes the canoe manageable by four people. Since the four can be at the ends of the canoe, the whole entourage can ease through a much narrower trail. Either way, with four or six bearers, don't try this method for more than a couple of hundred yards. People start stumbling and get careless when they tire, and tempers get short. The distance should be no more than they can carry without stopping to rest.

Gear

Moving gear across a portage is what caused me to develop the trip boxes that I build and use. Earlier on, I tried the boxes that many canoe trippers use. Most of these have a handle or handles on each end and are built for two people to carry by hand. I found these very uncomfortable and tiring to carry over a long portage—they bumped the legs and were very difficult to manage, especially on a narrow trail. Yet the weight in these boxes is seldom more than one person could comfortably carry on the back. So, I built my boxes to the backpacked by one person. Some canoe trippers I have met proudly point out how nicely their boxes fit into the canoe. My boxes fit onto a person! I always have plenty of room in the canoe, but people only have two hands. If they can get the heavy gear comfortably on the back, then the hands are free to carry small stuff like spare paddles, camera bags etc.

I went to a canoe show several years ago where we displayed some of the cedar strip canoes we build. At the last minute, I decided to take along a couple of trip boxes we had just finished to display

For short carries get the crew together and carry it loaded.

Easily-carried boxes take much of the drudgery out of portaging.

along with the canoes. I was surprised to find that many serious canoe people were more interested in the waterproof, backpackable trip boxes than in the canoes.

The longer the portage, the more important it is that as few trips as possible be made by each person. Two people traveling light can portage in one trip—one carries the canoe and one light pack, and the other carries the heavier of the packs. However, on most trips with groups I find it necessary for everyone to make two trips, and a few have to make a third. If everyone makes a one-person carry (something that almost never happens), then only two trips per person are needed. The normal canoe load is one food box and the two personal packs. These make three portaging loads, and the canoe makes four. If the two people team up on the canoe, there will be second trip for both and a third for one.

No matter how many trips he makes, the leader should plan to be at the starting point when the last of the gear is picked up, to ensure that nothing is left behind. If you cannot do this, designate a responsible person to do it for you. This is important to prevent leaving essential (and expensive!) equipment behind. Something like a tent might not be missed until it is time to set up camp many miles down the river.

Some Tips

Most portage trails are well worn and it would seem impossible to wander from them, but Thoreau did it and don't think your people won't. Unless you are sure the trail is well defined and marked, you should be the first one over it so as to clearly mark any place where they could possibly go wrong. Don't depend on them staying within sight of you. This does not work; people carrying a load have to move at their own pace. A few minutes spent marking the trail with some previously agreed-upon signal is well worth while, and can save hours of searching for lost people.

For long carries I use a little incentive that works especially well with kids, but I think is just as effective with adults, although they will not admit it. I am the first one across the carry, so I leave a snack there for them, usually candy bars or other high energy food. It is like dangling the carrot in front of the donkey, and any 11-year-old can see through it, but it works! They remind me not to forget it on the next trip across.

An age-old method of getting a loaded canoe through difficult or unrunnable rapids is to line it—that is, to control the canoe from shore using the bow and stern lines. Lining is a valuable technique to the canoe traveler and has saved me countless hours of unpacking and repacking. However, I do not always allow my guests to line their canoes. The reason is this: Until they have had enough experience with a canoe in moving water to realize how quickly even a mild current can turn and upset it, they are not ready to control one with lines. Merely holding one line taut when it should be allowed to go slack will turn the canoe broadside so quickly that even an alert partner cannot stop it. This can happen much faster with lines than when the canoe is being handled with paddles. Over-control is the most common error: Not content to let well enough alone, they'll tug on the line(s) and pull the canoe around when it was doing just fine by itself.

Of course, if the trip is lengthy enough, and I expect many areas where the canoes could be lined, then instruction and practice in proper lining technique would be undertaken. But if it is just a solitary section that I feel is best not to run, I'll demonstrate the lining technique with my own canoe and then help with theirs one at a time. This gives them some experience, working with me, and—hopefully—we get through without an upset.

I think that, through the years, I have seen as many canoes upset while lining with inexperienced people as in running rapids.

Few people look forward to a portage, no matter how long or short it may be, but the willingness to undergo the hardships can bring one to those beautiful, quiet and uncrowded waterways that are not accessible by any other way. The overall satisfaction and lasting memories one obtains from a successful canoe trip are always enhanced by the difficulties of a portage. For the young people, there is a good lesson in the value of stick-to-it-iveness: When there is no other way to get the gear from one place to another, they find they can do it.

Poling

In the nineteenth and early twentieth centuries, the guest sat in the front of the canoe with nothing to do except sit with folded hands and enjoy the scenery. The guide provided all of the propulsion and steering, and, almost to a man, the guides preferred to do it with a pole instead of a paddle. They'd resort to paddling only when the water got too deep for the pole.

These old-timers would roll over in their graves if they could see modern-day guides running down rapids full-tilt with the guest in the bow drawing left and right as they help to steer the loaded canoe through rocks, chutes and haystacks. But today's canoe trippers expect to be participants, not just riders, and this fact has led to a declining use of the setting pole by many guides as well as by most serious canoe travelers. There are times, though, when familiarity with the use of a pole can come in handy—especially for the leader, but for the guests as well. If you have not yet tried poling, you should! There will come a time when you'll be glad you did. Besides, it is fun, and it makes you *and* your canoe a lot more versatile.

Get a book and do a little reading; then, go out and do a lot of practicing, both upstream and down. Like paddling, poling seems to come naturally after a few tries, and then you just require more practice to become proficient. Bill Riviere's *Pole, Paddle & Portage* (Van Nostrand Reinhold Co., New York, 1969) has an excellent chapter on poling, and there should be no need to read further unless you get hooked on competitive poling.

The easiest and fastest way upstream—the pole.

For downstream work, I have found two types of situations where I have needed to use my pole: taking a loaded canoe through solo, and taking a loaded canoe through very shallow stretches of river or streams.

The old-time guide used the pole for descending rapids because he had to go it alone. His "sport" was expected to sit still, and that was all! Once in a while, for one reason or another, a party will lose a person. The cause could be sickness, trouble at home, or any number of reasons. This means that the most experienced member of the group (the guide or leader) must carry on alone with the loaded canoe. On the few occasions that this has happened to me, I have been very thankful for my setting pole and the knowledge of how to use it.

The pole allows one to stop the canoe almost anywhere. This gives time to read the river, to align the canoe and avoid bumping rocks. Because you are standing, you have a good view ahead and can pick your way along with none of the apprehension that sometimes goes with running a fully loaded canoe through rapids with paddles.

In shallow water, both bow and stern paddlers find themselves stabbing at the bottom with their paddles in their efforts to maneuver the canoe, slow it down and align it with the narrow chutes and passages. In this situation, the stern person should be on his or her feet with the setting pole in hand while the bow paddler assists by pulling the front to the left or right as needed. There is just no way to descend some of those small, fast-running streams with paddles without climbing a rock every two or three minutes. The water, and thus the canoe, goes too fast to allow any time for maneuvering in the small space available. Back-paddling is out in this situation because the water is too shallow for you to get a "bite" with the paddle blade.

It is much more pleasant (and professional-looking) to ease the canoe down through these difficult areas with a pole. When room and water depth are sufficient the canoe can be allowed to shoot ahead with the current. Then when the passage narrows again, a couple of snubs with the pole will slow or halt forward progress.

For upstream work, there are two possibilities: either get out and wade, dragging the canoe along behind; or pole. At first, it always seems like wading and dragging are faster and easier than poling, but this just isn't so. Whenever I have taken groups into areas where upstream work was needed, I have found myself, and those who mastered the fundamentals of poling, spending many hours a day waiting for the waders to catch up. (There are always some who just won't try.)

Poling a canoe upstream is not as difficult as it may seem, especially if the bow person helps to steer the canoe by drawing right or left as the stern person provides the forward motion by poling. Most times the guests try poling, then wading, before they climb back into the canoe, vowing to master the pole.

You may find yourself heading up an adventurous group that wants to ascend to some remote wilderness lake for its fantastic fishing, or maybe just to climb the river "because it is there." Whatever the reason, a good ten- or twelve-foot pole for each canoe will be needed. Get the guests out beforehand and let them get the feel of propelling a canoe with a pole. A few hours of practice before starting up a stream does wonders for the confidence. An upstream trip should be limited to experienced paddlers, and you will find them eager to learn the ins and outs of poling. Mostly, you'll just have to put the pole in their hands and turn them loose.

There is another side to poling a canoe. Standing in the canoe opens whole new vistas—twice as much of the surrounding terrain is visible as would be from a canoe seat. Once the canoeist proves to himself or herself that the old myth about never standing in a canoe is just that—a myth—he/she will find a whole new dimension in canoeing.

For you, as guide, the increased visibility from an erect position allows you to lead your group through the best passages in white water, to spot and point out wildlife and interesting features, and to be prepared to handle your canoe alone, if necessary. The pole becomes a necessity instead of a handy accessory.

Outboard Motor

On every canoe trip, I *consider* whether or not to take along my little three horsepower outboard motor. There are times when I check it off and leave it at home and others when I consider it a necessity to have along. I do not run any motorized trips, so when it goes, it goes as a "just in case" sort of thing.

As I have mentioned, most people have a set number of days to spend on a canoe trip; they expect to get home on time to meet their work commitments or other obligations. When I feel the available time is just barely adequate to complete the trip, I take along the motor. This way, if we are delayed by headwinds or for other reasons we can make up time, or, in some cases, travel into the wind by using the motor. The outboard rides with its bracket and gas tank in the bottom of my canoe, and on most of these outings it is never used. But it is a comfort to me to have it, as an ace-in-the-hole, if needed.

When my guests include elderly or very young people about whom I have doubts as to whether or not they can keep up sustained paddling, I take along the motor. These folks enjoy the security of knowing they don't *have* to push themselves to the limit every day, and also they like the security of knowing I can quickly go for help or transport them rapidly in case of a medical emergency. But, unless needed, the motor gets a free ride.

Sometimes a group dislikes the idea of miles of paddling across lakes, but wants to enjoy paddling the river portions of a particular trip. Here, the motor can be used for the flatwater and stored when

A small outboard motor can be an important tool for the guide.

on the river.

I have found that I can tow four or five canoes with that little three-horsepower motor at about the same speed as the canoes would travel if paddled by the two occupants. This means that the group will not travel any faster at any given time, but the motor can maintain the pace hour in and hour out. Over the course of several hours, the group will be miles ahead of where it would have been by paddle power alone.

Towing a string of canoes is suited only to larger bodies of water where there is no need for close turns or precise maneuvering. Caution the people, especially active youngsters, about not moving around and doing anything that might capsize a canoe. It would be quite a mess to be all strung together with a canoe, gear and people in the water. Use good judgment and common sense!

The outboard can be an important part of the trip leader's equipment, and at times I consider it a necessity. At other times, it would just be excess baggage and unnecessary insurance. Also, people might resent having it along. Give each trip separate consideration evaluating the needs, desires and abilities of the people concerned.

5 Wet Weather

Rain is a paradox for the canoeist. Without it, canoes soon grind to a halt on sand and gravel bars. Once-easy stretches of Class I and II rapids become minor riffles that must be waded, dragging the canoe behind. On what were otherwise easy, carefree passages, it becomes an irritating challenge to find enough water to float a canoe. On the other hand, when the rain *does* come, the canoeist's main focus of attention becomes one of keeping self and critical equipment dry, and considerable energy is expended toward these ends. Canoeing *and* camping become complicated. So, even though the rain causes problems, the canoeist must accept it philosophically and learn to cope with it. The canoeist's dream: rainy nights spent in the tent, clear sunny days on the water. Ah, what a life.

When a canoe party is besieged with a steady rainfall, with low-lying clouds closed in all around and no sign of let-up, people tend to get edgy and discouraged. They start feeling that it surely will never end, and that the only way to escape being continuously soaked is to quickly finish the trip and get home.

No one likes being wet, and no one wants a long-awaited canoe vacation to be shrouded in cloudy, overcast weather. Where is the bright blue sky with the puffy white clouds that was thought of so many times in anticipation of this outing? The trip leader must do everything possible to minimize the discouraging effects of inclement weather, and to make the people realize that rain too is part of the trip and he is prepared for it.

I had a party of two German families from Dusseldorf, West Germany, on the Allagash one summer. During a very bleak, damp, showery day they assured me that this type of weather was of no consequence to them. They were prepared for it and, besides, in Dusseldorf they were accustomed to weeks of just that kind of weather. (Indeed, I remember such weeks during my service days in Germany.) Still, when the sky cleared, they cheered the sunshine and dry air like everyone else on the river. The point is, no one "gets used" to rain. We learn to live with it.

Their cheerful acceptance of the inevitable made my job easier, to be sure, but they still had to be shown how to stay as dry and comfortable as possible without the benefit of a solid roof over their heads. One day, I remember, we were setting up camp under the threat of rain. I was busy elsewhere and did not see one couple set their tent over a comfortable-looking hollow in the ground. When the rain came, it came in torrents! Within minutes, the hollow filled up and the bottom of the tent was like a water bed.

Had I seen the site they had selected beforehand, I would have warned them off, but with the tent up it could not be seen. Everything worked out all right in this case because the sun came out a little later. We moved the tent, and the nylon floor quickly dried out. However, had the rain continued it would have been a real problem getting things dry enough for them to sleep in the tent comfortably.

You have the responsibility of seeing to it that the group is as comfortable as possible under all circumstances. This is done by being prepared for rain before starting the trip, knowing how to cope with it when it comes, and putting forth that extra effort to make everyone as comfortable as possible.

Advance Preparation

Advance preparation for wet weather means that you seriously and realistically *plan* to get rained on; treat rain as though it were *bound* to happen. While these circumstances are certainly not so pleasant to contemplate as the nice clear, warm, easy-going days on the water, it is the lot of the trip leader to think about such things, and to prepare for them.

There are three separate areas of consideration: 1) the rain gear each person carries, 2) the tents where they will sleep, and 3) a tarp to provide a dry place for a kitchen-eating-gathering area. With these things provided, the trip leader has done all he can, other than exuding realistic optimism.

Your optimism and attitude can be contagious. One summer, on a nine-day river trip with a family of five, we were dampened by three days of cloudiness and intermittent drizzle. With each successive shower I cheerfully predicted that it was a "clearing shower." I still get an occasional card or note from them, never failing to chide me about our three days of "clearing showers." Still, the attitude set the mood for cheerful acceptance of what could not be helped, and, while my ability as a weather forecaster may have been seriously questioned, my preparedness for the situation was not.

Personal Wet Weather Gear

The choice of personal rain gear is just that, personal, I cannot really say that I have found one type or style really superior over another in all respects. The rainsuit, pants and jacket, will afford the best all-over protection, and this is what I personally carry. The big disadvantage is the inconvenience of putting on the rain pants. In showery weather this is a real pain in the neck, and I don't put the pants on in these circumstances unless the weather is cold. The jacket keeps my top dry, and I allow my legs to get wet.

An ordinary raincoat is what most people have, and this is perfectly all right for summertime use. A raincoat provides the necessary protection to the top part of the body and will cover the legs while paddling. The lower legs will get wet, but this can be lived with; wet pant legs will usually dry out while their owner is standing around the campfire later on.

I discourage the use of ponchos. They are just the thing for the backpacker, I guess, but not so for the canoeist. I always shudder when I think what might happen to someone wearing a poncho in a canoe upset. All of that material tangled up around the arms and legs would make swimming impossible, unless the person was lucky enough to get the poncho off.

The cagoule is a good choice for wet weather canoeing, but it is a specialized garment, one that a person is not likely to have, nor would he or she be eager to lay out the cash needed to buy one for a single canoe trip.

Once you are satisfied that all your people have the necessary gear to keep their bodies dry, turn your attention to the feet. People accustomed to walking from building to building on a paved surface do not have the necessary experience to know how to care for their feet on a canoe trip.

My own choice of footgear is the Maine Hunting Shoe manufactured and sold by L.L. Bean (Similar combination leather-rubber boots are marketed by other makers.) Actually, I use two pair: For everyday use I have a low, shoe-height pair. In wet weather, or if I get the low ones wet, I have an eight-inch pair that keep my feet dry in the wettest of weather.

The worst footgear I have ever seen in my life for canoe tripping is the most popular, especially with kids. I'm talking about the suede, padded nylon sneaker/jogging shoe. These things just plain refuse to dry out once they have been soaked. Three days of sunny bluebird weather might do it, but when the weather is overcast these shoes will end up piled around the campfire; and I don't believe I have ever seen a pair completely dried out this way. Then, there is the burning up of the tops, melting of the soles, overall scorching, and any combination thereof. These shoes are expensive, and my Yankee thrift revolts at this waste. Anyway, the popularity of these things keeps them coming, and I get the feeling that I may as well try to stop the rain from coming down or the river from flowing as to try to stop people from wearing them.

For a second set of footgear, insist that people bring something waterproof, or nearly so. Feet are going to get wet on a canoe trip whether it rains or not. Constantly wet feet are *not* a pleasure.

Tents

The variety of good, lightweight tents on the market today is tremendous. As long as the quality is good, most any of them are perfectly adequate for canoe camping. My own choice is a nylon tent with a very generous fly that extends over the tent in all directions. This large fly not only keeps the tent itself (which, for breathability, is not waterproof) dry but sheds the water far enough away from the floor so that there is little danger of water running under the tent. Mine have stood the test of time and constant use, and I am satisfied with them. They are sold by L.L. Bean, and are called Allagash Tents.

I provide tents for my guests. I use four-person tents, but for two people—anyone who has crowded into a two-person tent with a companion will appreciate the extra space. Packs and personal gear

The tarp offers refuge from sudden showers as well as steady downpours. Note the use of food packs as tie-downs, instead of stakes.

can be taken inside and there is still plenty of room for two people to sleep.

In wet weather, what's more important than the kind of tent used is *how* it is used. (This is covered later in this chapter, under *Sleeping Area.*) Before packing for the trip, be sure all tents are checked at home for completeness and damage; you don't want to overlook a needed repair that you postponed at the end of last season. If the people in your party are bringing their own tents, ask that they do the same.

The Tarp

Next to the tents, the rain tarp is the most important piece of rain protection equipment you can carry for your people. Don't leave home without it!

Camp life can be unbelieveably dull if the tents are the only shelter from an unceasing rain. For one thing, the people are forced to separate into small cliques of two or three, so the camaraderie of the group suffers and can be lost altogether. Secondly, the best of camp cooks cannot prepare a decent meal with the rain pouring down, drenching the stove, the fire, and generally wetting things that are not supposed to be wet.

My tarp is made of waterproofed nylon and measures about 12 feet by 14 feet. The size is barely adequate, and I often wish I had a larger tarp or another to extend the one I have. The nylon rolls up so compactly that not having room for a tarp is the weakest of excuses for not having one along. Mine makes a roll about one foot long and four or five inches in diameter with the ropes attached.

Four or six mil polyethylene plastic will make a perfectly adequate rain tarp, and for a fraction of the cost of nylon. It is a little more bulky, but otherwise works perfectly. To attach tie-down ropes, place small stones three or four inches from the edge of the plastic, wrap the poly around it, then tie it with the rope. It will take a hurricane to tear it loose.

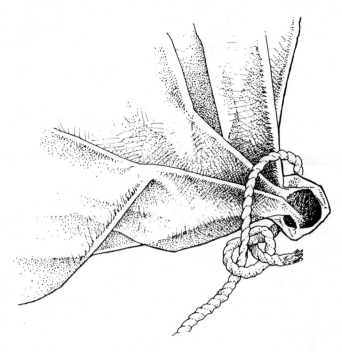

Home-made tarp of polyethylene. Tie rocks in corners for rip-free attachment of ropes.

Once you have assured yourself that all personal equipment and camping equipment are adequate for any weather and everything is packed away in waterproof containers (making them is covered in the final chapter), your mind can be at ease. You'll know that you have done everything possible to ensure the comfort of your group. Now, like life insurance, hope that you don't have to use it.

Coping En Route

The trip leader worthy of the title will put forth the extra effort that is needed to make everyone as comfortable as possible when the sky is grey and people's dispositions are not much brighter. The decisions you must make will depend somewhat on the experience of your group, but, nevertheless, your directions will be required and expected.

Pulling into camp after a wet day of paddling is not usually done with the same enthusiasm as on a clear pleasant day. If the group is really inexperienced, call them together for a quick meeting and tell them what has to be done. Don't be sickeningly cheerful about the whole thing, but show that it is not an unusual situation and that you know what to do to make the best of it. Lay the work out so that everyone is busy until the camp is set up and comfortable. People standing around in the rain with nothing to do will just become more and more miserable with self-pity.

The rainy day camp has two major areas from the individual's point of view. The first is his or her own tent; a warm place to sleep is of paramount importance. The second is the kitchen area where the group can get together and socialize, eat and stay dry.

Sleeping Area

As good night's sleep is of vital importance to everyone. Without the comfort of a dry, warm tent and sleeping bag, restful sleep is nearly impossible. Above all else (with the possible exception of food), the sleeping bag should be kept dry. Being totally soaked all day is bearable if one can look forward to a warm, restful night's sleep.

The fewer trips into and out of a tent the people make during rainy weather, the drier it will remain. One way to avoid a lot of trips in and out is to keep the personal packs on the outside. It is easy to keep them dry: Just lean the pack frame against a convenient tree, and pull a large plastic trash bag down over it. It will stay dry, keep the tent uncluttered, and is a lot easier to get at when something is needed from it. The bag can be folded up and slipped into the pack for traveling or can be used over the pack in the canoe if the rain persists.

The type and quality of the tents is important, but even more important is how they are used. Inexperienced people should be shown the best areas for their tents. A smooth, hard packed, level area, much used and free of vegetation, may look like an ideal place if it happens to be dry at the time. However, the lack of vegetation allows water to spread out on the surface and eventually spread under the tent floor. Even the most waterproof nylon material is apt to become damp on the inside after a night of this constant soaking.

I have already mentioned the folly of pitching tents in a hollow. For some reason, these hollows always seem secure and inviting. Other than being bowl-shaped with no place for water to go, they seem perfect: comfortably curved, smooth, and with a nice carpet of grass.

When the tents have to be taken down and rolled up in wet weather, the chance of the *entire* tent becoming wet is increased. While this cannot be avoided, it can be minimized by careful handling and attention to detail. If possible, wait for a lull in the rain and get the tents packed up as quickly as possible. If the weather is clearing, they will quickly dry out once they are put up again at your destination, but if the weary weather continues, the careful handling must continue.

(Incidentally, the best way to dry a wet tent is to set it up. Don't try to hang it out.)

One final thought to pass along on tent care: keep it off the bottom of the canoe. Even during dry weather it is liable to rest in water that splashes in. This is not serious on fair days because the tent will quickly dry when set up again, but after you have carefully kept a tent at least semi-dry in foul weather it would be a shame to soak it through careless handling in the canoe.

The Kitchen-Social Area

The tiny island created by the tarp, with a cheery warm fire going, is among the most important morale boosters you can provide. Things never seem as bad, somehow, when the fire is going and there is a dry place to gather with friends. People will often start talking with a hint of pride in what they have come through and how they are coping with it. As long as they talk this way, your job is easy. Just see to it that their success continues.

The geography of every campsite is different, and there are many ways of putting up the tarp. It should cover the eating-cooking area and extend over the campfire enough to keep most of the rain from reaching it. Be sure that it is high enough so that neither the fire nor sparks will burn it, and that it is secure enough not to blow away or sag too low as it gets wet.

The Campfire

One cool rainy afternoon, I was standing around a blazing fire with a group of young people from a summer camp in Maine. We had been there for about two hours and were warm and dry in spite of the drizzle that had been falling all day. We watched another group pull into the area and proceed to set up camp. In a while, one of the leaders came over to me and asked, "Where'd you get the dry wood?" I'm not sure to this day whether he thought that dry wood was provided by some beneficial authority and all he had to do was find out where it was stored, or if he was asking me to explain how to obtain wood from the forest. Anyway, in my confusion, not sure if he was serious or not, I guess I may have been kind of rude. I pointed at the woods and said, "It's all around you." As I remember, he didn't look very enlightened as he walked away.

First a curl of birch bark as dry as it can be,
Then some twigs of softwood, dead, but on a tree,
Last of all some pine-knots to make the kittle foam,
And there's a fire to make you think you're setting' right at home.

ERNEST THOMPSON SETON, *The Book of Woodcraft*

The dry wood *is* all around. Unless it has been raining for two or three days, the dead limbs (squaw wood) on the lower branches of fir, spruce and pine trees will be quite dry, as they are protected from direct rain by their canopy of live boughs overhead. If the rain has been coming down long enough to wet the squaw wood then the problem is more serious, but still no call for a cold camp.

Standing dead fir and spruce trees as well as cedar in some areas are usually abundant in most northern canoe areas. No matter how long it has been raining, the wood *inside* these trees will be dry. All you have to do is cut them up and carefully split off the wet outer wood, then split up and set aside the nice dry wood from the inside. Don't discard the wet stuff; once you have a good hot fire going, this wet wood will dry out and sustain the blaze.

Most well-used campsites along rivers have been pretty well cleaned of nearby dry wood. Don't let this discourage you. Most campers seem to have an invisible line beyond which they will not travel for wood; usually 100 to 150 yards is the limit. This seems like a long way to most people in the woods, but it is really no trouble to drag a dead four-or-five-inch-diameter spruce or fir that distance. Cut it up at the fireplace to your favorite lengths.

Another good source of dry firewood for the canoeist is the "dri-ki" that accumulates on the islands found in the courses of most rivers. During spring runoff, driftwood piles up on the upstream ends of these islands, and during the summer, after baking in the sun, it is hard to beat as fuel. Just stop, pick up a few pieces of a convenient size and length, and lay them in the canoes atop the gear. When you get to camp, all you have to do is cut it up, and your firewood worries are over for the day.

Dry hardwood is hard to find in Maine, where my canoeing is done. The rivers flow through spruce-fir forest and there just are not many hardwoods around, much less dry ones. Many books and camping publications make too much fuss over the need for hardwood for the campfire. The fact is that if dry hardwood trees are not there, then you must use what is available. What is available is what is most abundant—in my case, spruce and fir. However, if you choose to pick up from the islands, you'll have the best chance to find dry hardwood. Most of the wood will be soft woods, but variety can be found—and all dry. You may not be able to identify the species after it has dried and bleached in the sun for months or years, but who cares? Just the heft of it will tell you that it is good, solid, long-burning hardwood. These island woodpiles almost always serve up some dry cedar or dry pieces of alder (called "biscuit wood" by old-timers because of its quick hot fire). These woods will produce a bright blaze for the reflector oven or can be set aside for kindling.

Once the dry wood is ready to go you will need some sort of tinder to get it burning. There are several kinds available, and a few tricks to go along with them.

Birch bark is the best possible fire starter that is available to the camper. It is always my first choice. White birch trees near campsites are frequently and thoughtlessly stripped to their inner bark by campers with knives, hatchets and axes. Don't allow this. A five-minute stop at a birch stand at an anomymous spot along the river will produce enough bark for an entire trip. Just stuff it into a bag and wedge it under a canoe seat. Don't cut the bark from the

With the sky threatening, keep gear covered and raincoats handy.

tree, but the loose pieces that can be pulled off by hand will do absolutely no damage to the tree. There will also be pieces scattered around on the ground that have fallen off naturally.

If the weather is really wet, you can supplement the resin in the birch bark with that of the fir tree. Take a knife and break the blisters in the bark. Spread the pitch on your kindling. Again, get out of camp to collect this stuff. Although collecting it does no harm to the tree, it is messy to touch and does not look too good.

I keep matches in a waterproof container tucked away in my gear, but for day to day use I carry one of those disposable butane lighters. (Don't dispose of them in the fire, or—bang!) Water does not damage them. Body heat will dry them out after a dunking, but the best feature, as far as wet weather fires is concerned, is the sustained adjustable flame that is much appreciated when everything is damp.

The campfire is *so* important. Not only during wet weather, but as the social center for a night in the woods. The fondest memories of past trips invariably include the time spent around the evening campfire. Whether what happens is idle talk, singing or lively discussion of the day's events, the fire is the physical object that brings the people together. The spiritual bonds develop naturally between them and will be permanent.

Afloat in the Rain

If you have ample time and your schedule allows for some lay-over days, you may want to consider using one to stay at camp on a rainy day. It is easier to keep everything dry if the camp is left standing during a rain than if it is broken down and set up again at a new location. Unfortunately, this luxury is often not possible.

When stowing their gear in the canoe, the people must take the time to carefully ensure that everything wettable is kept off the canoe bottom. This can be done by placing sticks under these items or placing the wettable atop the non-wettable. Packs, sleeping bags and tents should be covered with plastic trash bags and double-checked to make sure that they are not near the floor where accumulated water will surely soak them. Don't depend on trash bags to keep out standing water—they are too thin, and quickly develop pin holes that allow water to seep in.

A little common sense, attention to detail, and care will ensure that your party will move from one campsite to the next without any serious wetting of people or gear.

I have had guests remark to me, "You know, the river is really beautiful in the rain." It *is* beautiful. It is a mood. This mood is apart from what the average canoeist sees, even though he or she is right there. You have to look for the beauty, but it is there—waiting.

6 For Their Enjoyment

> "Look here!" said the Water Rat. "If you've really nothing else on hand this morning, supposing we drop down the river together, and have a long day of it?"
> The Mole waggled his toes from sheer happiness, spread his chest with a sigh of full contentment, and leaned back blissfully into the soft cushions. "What a day I'm having!" he said. "Let us start at once!"
> KENNETH GRAHAME, *The Wind In the Willows*

This is what it is all about. This is why the people are out there with you, for the sheer enjoyment of it. Do whatever you can to show them *how* to enjoy it.

You cannot expect people to step from one environment to another and instantly have a full appreciation for what is there or how to go about enjoying it. Appreciation cannot be spoon-fed, but you can suggest, show by example, and inform. The appreciation will come to some and not to others, and this is to be expected.

I like to think that I am doing my part as an educator as well as a guide, becuase as people develop an appreciation and understanding of wild places they are apt to be more intelligent voters about matters concerning wilderness areas and the environment.

Any photographers in the group are usually already interested in their surroundings. The serious photographer quickly realizes the importance of knowing and understanding the subject to be photographed; this is the route to maximum enjoyment for these people. Photographers keep a guide on his or her toes as they constantly ask questions about their subjects.

The questions most frequently asked by canoe trippers concern wildlife. Most people are captivated by animal sightings and consider these the highlights of their trip. The guide, with his or her knowledge of wild animals and their habits, can help make sightings (and dealings) with wild animals totally enjoyable.

Years ago, before our children came along, my wife and I visited Rome. We didn't have much money, so I quickly refused offers of local guides to show us the Forum, the Colosseum, etc. However, as we wandered around and looked at this fascinating place, we found ourselves hungering for information about it. I took pictures, but didn't know of what. Finally, we returned to a well-dressed gentleman who had offered his services, and hired him.

We retraced our route with the guide, and the second time it was as if we had not been there before. His knowledge brought new meaning to the place for us. His descriptions gave life to the ruins. I could see returning Roman legions marching triumphantly down the Appian Way, with the chariots rattling over the cobblestones and the horses' hooves ringing out sharply. I could vividly imagine the crowded Colosseum as the bloodthirsty crowd cheered gladiators in their fight to the death.

We hired our guide for a second day to see another part of the city. I have no idea now what we paid him, but, whatever it was, it was money well spent. I want my guests to feel this same way when their trip with me is over. I try to make them "see" the wilderness. There's a lot more to it than just taking them there, feeding and looking after them.

And yet, each person has his/her own experience. Some people may be brimming over with fun and enjoyment; there may be someone apparently sulking about something that has nothing to do with you (or the trip); and some people just keep to themselves. I've learned to not be *too* anxious about my guests.

One woman in a small group of canoeists was acting very withdrawn and quiet. She spent long periods of time alone, and when she was with others she didn't have much to say. I was concerned about her and wondered if I or someone else had said or done something to offend her. However, I didn't feel I knew her well enough to ask her what was wrong. Eventually, as we became better accquainted, the lady came to me and said, "This is the most fantastic experience I have ever had."

Of course, I was surprised and relieved to hear this, and I learned something from it: I learned that you can't always tell what people are thinking by how they act. What I was mistaking for sulking and dissatisfaction in this person was actually a deep and personal sense of appreciation that she could not express to a stranger. I'm glad we became friends.

Appreciation

It is late afternoon, and my daughter and I are paddling slowly and silently through the water trails that wind through a hugh marsh. The sun is low in the sky as evening approaches, and it is warm, yet not uncomfortable. The only sounds are the subtle ones that require the mental re-tuning of our auditory systems to appreciate—The splashing walk of a feeding moose in the distance, the quick movement of an unidentified animal scurrying through the tall grass, the faint gurgle of marsh gas escaping to the surface of the water.

Wildlife is everywhere we look. We glide slowly along, and see the white-cheeked faces of a family of Canada geese peering apprehensively at us through the tall grass as we pass. Rounding a corner we surprise another family group swimming; they quickly disappear into the surrounding vegetation, where they too wait for us to go by.

Later, we spot the V-shaped wake of a muskrat swimming across a small pond within the marsh. He sees us and dives, not to be seen again, but we know he has surfaced in the grass and bushes, waiting for the strange, elongated creature with two heads to leave his pond.

On the far side of the same pond, a cow moose stands in water up to her belly. Her head is submerged while she feeds on the aquatic vegetation growing on the bottom. Finally, her head comes up, with water running off her drooping ears and splashing into the pond; she chews, breathes and looks around at her surroundings to note any changes that may have taken place during the minute or so her head was under the water. We are still some distance away, and the

slight breeze is blowing from her to us; she hasn't noticed us. Her attention frequently turns to a small grass hummock near the water's edge, and I whisper to my daughter to watch it closely for a calf that is probably hidden there.

While her head is down, we paddle directly toward her. When it comes up, we freeze and allow the canoe to drift. The calf sees us first and nervously leaves its hiding place to move out to join its mother. The adult spots us as we approach to within fifteen or twenty yards. But, there is no panic-striken flight to cover. The large animal looks us over and finally decides she would be more comfortable with a shield of vegetation between us. She moves with an unconcerned, almost casual attitude toward shore. Her calf follows close behind, but showing none of the aloofness of its mother.

Our interest in wildlife and the beauty of the evening create a mood which causes us to look, watch, and wait—to be alert to motion, to appreciate a fleeting glimpse of an animal with the same ardor as a long study. The smallest of the marsh animals can be as fascinating as the thousand-pound moose if the mind is attuned to them. We are completely absorbed, just sitting afloat on the shallow water, looking over the edge of the canoe, watching the minute animals scurry around. At first they seem to have no direction or purpose, but after a while their life patterns become a little more apparent, and we paddle away from the scene with a little more knowledge and appreciation than when we arrived.

Wild creatures, with their movement and variety, always attract attention and interest, but the marsh itself is beautiful and alive. As the sun dips down closer to the low-lying hills in the west, the grass, shrubs and the few trees that have managed to establish themselves are painted with the warm light of the setting sun. These plants of varying size, shape, shade and texture are placed in the marsh by the master hand—placed with the precision and harmony that no landscape architect could ever hope to achieve.

The breeze sways the tall marsh grass with subtle grace while the leaves on the low shrubs and bushes flutter, alternately exposing their dark upper surfaces, then their lighter-colored bottoms, to the fading late afternoon sun.

The beauty we see is actually a bonus, because we know this vegetation has several more important and practical functions in the ecology of the marsh. The most obvious is the haven it provides for the wildlife we have been watching. The leaves, branches and stems provide homes for countless birds and animals that inhabit the area. The roots are what hold the marsh soil together while the never-ending process of building continues, and more and more soil is added to the marsh, enriching it for future generations of plant and animal life.

With the sun almost touching the western tree line, we find ourselves in the deep hush of the evening. A time for reflection, for thought. I feel a deep contentment. There is nowhere I would rather be at this particular moment. Another canoe, two members of our party, are out on the marsh with us, and we can see from a distance that they too are caught up with the magic of the moment, moving slowly, if at all. Taking in every whisper of sound, every movement, every change in the fading light, they are with us in spirit and none of us will want, or need, to express in words to each other what we have experienced.

Suddenly, the quiet is shattered! A yell, followed by a roar of laughter, comes from the direction of our camp. Six of our party of ten are back there playing cards and apparently someone has just made a good play. Our reverie broken, we slowly start to paddle along the serpentine waterway leading through several minor channels to the main river where our camp is located.

This marsh that has given me many hours of quiet pleasure through the years is located at the foot of Chase Rapids on the Allagash River in northern Maine. It is the result of centuries—no, probably millennia—of siltation from the rushing, churning waters of the rapids suddenly slowed by the quiet waters of Umsaskis Lake. The process continues today, and this keeps the area alive, fertile, and viable.

I always welcome the opportunity to camp near this special area, not just for myself, but because it gives me an opportunity to introduce my guests to the wonders that it holds. Most are anxious to explore, and after a brief introduction to the area they move off independently and enjoy, as my daughter and I were doing.

Inspecting a bird's nest. The wilderness holds many wonders for those willing to look for them.

THE CANOE GUIDE'S HANDBOOK

Except for the two who were with us, this particular party was not interested in picking up a paddle again until it was time to move on down the river in the morning. They preferred to spend the remaining daylight playing cards, and they had a good time. But it always saddens me, this indifference to nature, because I know what they are missing. Unless they are receptive, though, I cannot communicate it to them. I would have been wrong to badger the card players to go, because if they did so just from a sense of duty or because they thought they were missing something, the whole thing would be meaningless to them. If they did not spot a moose or whatever they had expected to see, they would have considered the time wasted. They would be right! If people are unwilling to appreciate what is there, it is better to let it go at that.

This awareness is hard to communicate to someone who has not experienced it; if the person has, then communication is unnecessary. All one can do is try: Suggest the quiet paddle through the winding waterways, and hope people will reach that awareness, be caught up with it and become one of the lucky ones.

I think people have trouble shifting gears from life in the city or suburbs to life in a wilderness area and all that goes with it. Some people prepare themselves mentally ahead of time and are anxious to experience things such as I have described. Most, though, are accustomed to a sight-seeing type of tour and have trouble getting away from that attitude in eight or ten days.

One can visit the Statue of Liberty and find it just as expected; it will appear as pictured and will conform to written descriptions. A castle overlooking the Rhine—same thing, everything as expected. Nature, and the moods it provokes, are not as predictable, or as describable. We can try, as I have tried to describe an hour on Umsaskis Marsh, but each person who reads it will relate the description to his or her own experiences. Further, each visit will be different and evoke a different attitude and emotion in the observer.

Photography

I used to wonder at the number of people who go on canoe trips without taking a camera or, at least, without taking a *good* camera. I started questioning them and found that many of them were serious amateur photographers but did not want to risk losing or ruining their equipment. They risked missing once-in-a-lifetime photos because they didn't know what conditions to expect or how to protect their equipment.

I have been a photographer for many years and I *have* lost and damaged some equipment, but I have single photos in my files that I value many times over the cost of a good camera. The equipment can be replaced; a missed photo cannot!

Encourage your people to take their photo gear, but don't over-do your urging. If you are too insistent and then they *should* lose or damage it—well, you get the point.

There are several companies that manufacture plastic pouches especially for cameras and other delicate equipment. Not only are these waterproof, but they provide flotation and have the additional advantage of being padded so as to give the equipment some degree of protection from bumps and scrapes. Most outdoor equipment stores carry these pouches, and ads for them can be found in outdoor magazines.

For years I carried my photo gear in an old 50-caliber army surplus ammunition case. I padded the inside by contact-cementing foam rubber to the sides, bottom, and cover. This heavy steel box is almost indestructible, absolutely waterproof, and with a little padding will see equipment through an unbelievable amount of rough use and wet times. These boxes are available from army-navy surplus stores, and some sporting goods outlets carry them, as well.

When I outgrew my ammunition box, I built the watertight camera case shown in the photo. The construction method is the same as for the food packs described in the next chapter. The only difference is that I hinged the cover and paid a little more attention to the gasket to be sure it was as waterproof as possible. The box was filled with a block of foam rubber (the kind used for pillows), with cut-outs made to accommodate the cameras, lenses, and other items I seem not to be able to do without these days.

I think the leader owes it to the people in the group to at least point out how they could take along their valuable equipment with a minimum of risk. Go a little further and present the choice between the value of a once-in-a-lifetime picture and that of a two or three hundred dollar camera. Let them decide.

You don't have to be a photographer yourself to help others improve their picture quality. Remember, these people are in *your* bailiwick—you know it better than any of them. As an outdoor person you must have some favorite outdoor pictures. Relate these to the scenes your guests are trying to capture, and help them. I don't mean you will have to help them with the technical stuff—

The serious canoeist-photographer will need waterproof protection for equipment.

they will know how to handle the f-stops and shutter speeds—but help with framing, foreground interest, getting in close to the subject, interesting angles. Your suggestions can be a big help to them, and so can your experience as a guide.

One of the most common mistakes people make is trying to photograph an object from too far away. How many times have you looked at a photo with a wide expanse of water and sky and a thin tree line across the middle of it? The photographer points to a tiny spot along the tree line and proudly states that this is a picture of a deer. If the picture has to be explained, then the chances are it isn't too good. Try to get the picture takers as close as possible to the subject. Usually, the closer they can come to filling the whole frame with the moose, deer, or whatever, the better the photo will be. If they have telephoto lenses your job will be easier, but even then "the closer the better" is a good rule.

If your guests have just discovered the thrill of white water canoeing, they are going to want some pictures of themselves and others doing it. Help them by offering to take their cameras and shoot them running through a stretch that has a lot of waves and foam. Get as much "white" into the white water shot as possible. A low camera angle sometimes helps with this. Get down as close to water level as is practical, and try to take the picture as they hit the largest wave with the biggest splash. They'll love it!

It is often necessary, and worthwhile, to take the time to set up good white water pictures. No one has time to stop and take pictures on the initial run, so if the area has picture-taking possibilities, re-run them with some cameras on shore or in an eddy in mid-river. You don't need miles of white water to get good action shots. You

Close range (about one canoe length), plus a long lens, allowed me to get this detailed photo of a bull moose on a rainy day. He was feeding in water so deep that he disappeared completely when his head went down.

An unusual photo for me—I'm on the other side of the camera (in the stern). (Kathy Gilpatrick photo.)

may have the only thirty yards of white water in thirty miles of river, but the camera will isolate the action and could produce great pictures. As long as they are representative of the trip it makes no difference.

White water photography is going to take time, so plan ahead for it. There will be time needed to set up for one or more extra runs through an especially good stretch, plus the time needed to ensure the safety of equipment. Extra runs can be made without the gear that is normally carried. The absence of this dunnage will not be noticed in most pictures, and there will be less need for worry about upsets. Also, it is a lot more fun to run white water with an empty canoe that will respond instantly to the paddle.

Some of the best scenery in the world is found in canoe country, and people will want to photograph it. Most photographers have

Film is relatively cheap. Several exposures may be necessary to get the right combination of light and composition in a photograph like this.

experience with scenery and can handle it well. However, there are some things you can do to help out. One of the most common scenic pictures is the "I was there" photo in which the person or persons stand stiffly in front of the scene while someone snaps the picture. There are more subtle and pleasing ways to get the "I was there" photo.

Pictures of a beautiful sunset will convey the "I was there" idea if you get someone out on the water in a canoe. It doesn't matter who is paddling because all that will be seen in the picture is a silhouette. Another technique is to include part of the camp area in that "great scene." An overturned canoe on shore in the foreground, or the fireplace in the corner of the frame, will get across the idea that the person taking the picture was actually camped in the midst of all that beauty. It's the difference between a snapshot and a great picture.

Group pictures are important to everyone concerned. Keep them informal whenever possible. It may be necessary to pose for the group picture, but do it in a way that is natural and shows a usual activity. Your group will probably gather around the campfire in the evening: Use this natural gathering for group shots. It may be best to pose for it during daylight hours, but the shot will still depict a natural and usual activity. This makes it much more meaningful than a line-up in front of a canoe or whatever.

Almost everyone these days uses color film, either negative film for prints or positive film for slides. Professional outdoor photographers try to include a brightly colored object in their photos—"If you want to sell it, get some red in it." Brightly colored clothes, canoes, and equipment go a long way toward making color pictures more interesting and attractive.

Unusual conditions can make for striking shots. Here a combination of early morning fog and bright sky light make an unusual photo.

You, as leader, will be a favorite photo subject as you go about your chores in camp and while paddling on the river. My own canoe trip "uniform" is blue jeans and a bright red chamois cloth shirt with a "Registered Maine Guide" patch sewn on the left shoulder. I don't think being a photographer's model had any bearing on my original choice of outfit, but it has worked out well, keeps me recognizable, and gives them some bright color for their photographs.

Encourage to your people to take photographs. A picture can be such a great memory maker. Rough handling and moisture are the outdoor photographer's biggest enemies, but these dangers can be minimized and those wonderful times captured on film for a life time of enjoyment.

Wildlife

The cow moose was feeding in mid-stream as my party of young teen-agers rounded a bend in the slow-moving section of the river. A girl in the canoe next to me asked permission to move ahead for a closer photograph. I said okay, and the canoe moved forward. About the time their canoe was one canoe length in front of me and about three lengths from the moose, I noticed the moose look over her shoulder at a grassy island to our left front. I followed her look and saw her calf hidden in the grass and getting nervous about our presence. I immediately saw that the lead canoe was drifting directly between the cow and her calf. I called to them, and they changed course immediately.

As it turned out in this case, the cow was very calm about the whole thing. The feed must have been very good there, because she was reluctant to leave. In fact, she stayed there while her calf came splashing out to join her and then fidgeted around until, finally, they left together.

The unconcerned attitude of this female moose could be misleading, and there is the very real possibility that she would have quickly struck out at the canoe if she felt a threat to her young one. It is foolhardy to put one's self between *any* wild animal and her young. This applies to a thousand pound moose or a tiny squirrel weighing a few ounces. Each will fight to the death to protect its young, and each is surprisingly well-equipped to do it.

The trip leader deals with people whose experience with animals is usually limited to domestic pets or zoo animals. Neither experience equips them to deal with animals in the wild. However,

A more careful approach might have resulted in a better photograph.

observing and photographing the wildlife can be the highlight of most people's canoe trips. The leader has to see that they do it safely.

Every now and then a wild animal will appear to be completely tame. It will beg for food and completely captivate people to the point where they just *have* to pick the animal up. *Don't allow it!* Wild animals are not used to being handled and are liable to inflict serious injury in attempting to free themselves. Since you have no way of knowing anything about the health of the animal, you have to assume the worst.

Any animal bite will necessitate evacuation of the victim. The animal could be rabid or carrying other disease. If there is any way that you can kill the animal, you should do so. Evacuate the carcass with the victim so it can be examined by medical authorities. If it is a larger animal, send out the head. If you can do this it may save your guest from taking a series of painful rabies shots. Without the animal, the doctors will have to assume rabies and start immediate treatment.

Many of the more heavily used canoe routes have a population of resident camp raiders. Raccoons and black bears are the most common culprits, but skunks, squirrels, jays and others often take advantage of an easy meal. The only way to combat this problem is to do everything possible to remove the temptation.

Warn people not to eat in their tents nor to store *any* food there. In most cases of people being mauled by bears, the animal was searching not for people but for food it could smell. No container is tight enough to prevent an animal from smelling the food inside, so get food out of reach by hanging it where the animal cannot reach it or climb to it. My food packs have never been successfully broken into by any animal, but still, when I feel there is a good possibility of a nighttime raid, I hang them out of reach. Why ask for trouble?

Sometimes I am asked, "How come we don't see more animals?" My answer is almost always, "Because you make too much noise." How many animals are sighted depends on the type of people in the group. Some paddle along quietly and talk in hushed tones, and some move along yelling, singing and chiding one another. Both have a good time, and I'm not ready to criticize either type. However, I *do* feel it my responsibility to point out to the noisy ones why they are not seeing animals. Then it is up to them. If some of the group really want to observe wildlife, then peer pressure from them will take care of the others. Problem solved.

Most people will appreciate the sighting of a moose or deer or other large animal, but I feel it is important that I do what I can to help them enjoy the smaller, and more numerous, ones too. Make it a point to know something about the wildlife in your area. Often, a city person in my group has been amazed when told that a rabbit frequently seen hopping through our campsite is not a rabbit at all but a hare. (The varying hare, to be precise, and its color will change by November to snowy white.)

People delight in the nicknames of the Canada jays that flit about our area searching for hand-outs and scraps. "Whiskey jack," "gorbie," and "camp robber," they were called by old-time lumbermen; many a story is told of their raids on cooling pies and other undefended goodies around the cookshack.

It isn't unprofessional to take along books for wildlife identification. No one can be expected to know it all, and pertinent bits about a "just sighted" animal can make for fascinating reading.

The more you know about the animals, the more your guests will enjoy them. Make it your business to be as familiar with the wildlife in your area as you are with the area itself.

Coping with Insects

One type of wildlife causes more concern, frustration, and discomfort than any other, and it must be dealt with to ensure the total enjoyment of everyone in the party. Insects can completely ruin an otherwise perfect outing for someone who does not know how to handle the problem. They cannot (nor should they) be eliminated, so it is necessary to do everything possible to help folks cope with them.

As for myself, I'm lucky—years of exposure to black flies, mosquitoes, and (minges, no-see-ums, or whatever you call them) have had the happy result of making my body practically immune to their bites. I don't mean they leave me alone—they chew away on me just like everyone else—but I do not react to the bite by swelling or itching. Once the pest has done its thing, the episode is over. No after-effects.

In order to be sensitive to the problems of others in the insect department, I need only think back to my boyhood, when I was unknowingly building this immunity, and to the swelling, itching, and scratching I endured. I spent every spare minute in the woods and more often than not forgot to take the repellent along, if I had any to take. I still remember the constant itching and the scabs where I scratched off the swollen mosquito bites. My immunity has been built by a lifetime of exposure, and the early stages were not pleasant. People born and raised in the city or suburbs have no chance of having the least bit of immunity, but there are things that can be done to make the problem less severe and increase their comfort and enjoyment.

The most important insect protection is clothing. A circumstance that never fails to amuse me is the "outastater" (it's all one word here in Maine) who walks up wearing shorts and tee shirt, scratching and squirming and complaining about the bugs. The less skin left exposed, the less the problem! Advise your guests to have clothing that is heavy enough to deter the mosquitoes. A lightweight polyester shirt may be comfortable to wear and easy to keep clean, but a hungry mosquito will have no problem getting her proboscis through it.

If black flies are the problem, have everyone close up the cuffs of their shirts and pants. These pests are crawlers: they take great joy in getting halfway up the legs before starting to work. Tucking the trousers into the socks is effective for leg protection. Shirt cuffs can be buttoned and taped shut, and a bandanna around the neck is helpful. Some people find a head net to be just the thing for head protection. (I tried one once and decided I'd rather be bitten.)

They say the color of clothing has some bearing on the insect problem, and I guess it has been scientifically proven to be true. Don't count on a very noticeable effect, however. For what it is worth: Blue and purple seem to attract mosquitoes more than yellow or orange; bright colors repel them better than drab ones.

I'm often asked what kind of insect repellent I use. Rather than have them think I'm trying to be macho by saying "none," I give them a name brand and proceed to try to talk intelligently about their brand and others on the market. Actually, I do carry repellent with me and when bugs are extra thick I may put some on, but there are many summers when this happens only once or twice and some when I have not put any on at all.

Thoreau called his fly dope a "wash" and described it as follows:

It was composed of sweet-oil of turpentine, with a little oil of spearmint and camphor. However, I finally concluded that the remedy was worse than the disease. It was so disagreeable and inconvenient to have your face and hands covered with such a mixture.

Today's "washes" are not bad-smelling, are reasonably comfortable to wear, and they do a pretty good job, providing you are not looking for miracles. Be sure everyone carries a supply; you could have an extra bottle or two in case someone forgets or loses theirs. To really appreciate its effectiveness, one only has to go without it for a while when the insects are really thick.

Whenever I come home from a trip my wife kisses me and announces that I smell like a campfire. In this business it is a compliment, I guess, and the reason for it is that I spend a lot of time in wood smoke. Smoke is a natural repellent, and I find it far more pleasing than the kind I spread on my skin. The campfire will help keep the bug population down in the general campsite area, too. It doesn't take much wood to keep a smudge going, and it *does* make a difference. I think the smoke smell in the clothing makes a person less attractive to mosquitoes and black flies even when there is no fire going. It can't hurt!

I have heard it said, and seen it written, that taking vitamin B keeps insects from biting. Some people I know who have tried it swear by it, but I have always questioned the idea. Last year I had a man on a trip who was a medical doctor and a researcher. He told me that they showed vitamin B did indeed repel insects, but in order to be effective the doses had to be so massive that the body odor would keep away friends and family as well as insects. So much for vitamin B, but if you know someone who believes in it, don't burst his/her bubble. A good part of licking the insect problem is phychological, and if vitamin B helps, so be it!

Be sure the tents are insect proof. Nothing is worse than spending a hot, humid night swatting bugs instead of sleeping. When it is too hot inside the sleeping bag and too buggy outside, you can look for disgruntled guests at breakfast. Be sure all zippers work and that the nets are in good shape. If minges are a problem in your area, look for tents with netting fine enough to keep them out—they go right through ordinary window screen size netting. When these insects bite, the skin feels like it is afire. They attack with military precision: no one bites until the whole squadron is ready.

On those days when bugs are the worst, no one remedy will fully handle the problem. All you can do is combine all the things I have mentioned with any tricks of your own and then look forward to better times to come. One of the great things about canoe tripping is that the insects are minimal or non-existent on the water, so no matter how thick they are on land, there will always be relief on the water.

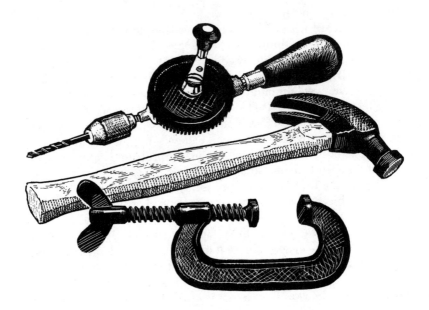

7 *Custom Gear*

Two tired, wet young men came ashore where we were camped, looking for a place to spend a rainy night. We were a group of twelve, and I suppose we appeared to completely fill the area. However, I assured them there was room in the rear and told them to feel free to carry their gear through our camp. They thanked me and started to move in. *That* turned out to be quite a process.

In all, they must have trudged through my camp at least ten or twelve times each. I know one made seven trips and the other eight *after* I noticed the more than usual amount of carrying they were doing. They were not friendly types, so I never got to know them, but I did wander around to look their gear over, both in the canoe and at the campsite.

The only thing I could figure was that they had started off with their food and camping gear packed in cardboard boxes. Once the trip was underway, the boxes disintegrated in the rain and left them without containers. If this was not the case, then these were two of the most disorganized human beings I have ever observed. The total time between their initial trip ashore and when they were set up and ready to cook supper was at least one and one half hours.

I returned to my tarp-covered fire and a hot cup of coffee feeling good about my packs and packing system. Each person in my groups makes *two trips* ashore to land everything needed to set up camp. This assumes that everyone carries a good load, of course; a third trip is usually needed to collect items that were pulled from packs during the day's travel and not repacked. If efficiency and speed are important, this third trip can be used to carry the canoes up and turn them over for the night.

The way to achieve this kind of efficiency is to have a container for everything that isn't large enough to be a load by itself. I do this with equipment I've designed and built to meet my needs. Included here are instructions for making three pieces of this gear of which I am particularly proud—the food packs, a kitchen pack, and a wooden pack frame. All of these can be made in a modestly equipped workshop.

Food Packs

The food pack shown in the drawing has nearly 4,000 cubic inches of usable space. These packs can be carried by hand, using the strap handles on the sides; this is usually best for making short trips from canoe to shore. The packs are also equipped with padded shoulder straps, and they can be back-packed. While they are certainly not as comfortable to carry as a well-designed pack frame would be, they are welcomed by anyone who has ever struggled over a portage trail with a traditional hand-carried canoe trip box. Some other things these boxes have going for them are: they are reasonably water-proof; they are rugged and stand the abuse of year-in, year-out use; they make great seats for gathering around the campfire. You can tie your rain tarp ropes to them if stakes are not quickly available, you can play checkers or chess on them, and they are animal-proof.

I didn't realize just how animal-proof these packs are until some friends told me of an experience they'd had while on a canoe camping trip; I had made them a pair of the packs, and they were using them for the first time.

Hat and Alice Souther were awakened early one morning to a commotion in the kitchen area of their campsite. They hitched their way, still in their sleeping bags, to the tent entrance and watched a full-grown black bear tearing, biting, swatting and generally mauling their food pack trying to get at its contents. After some minutes

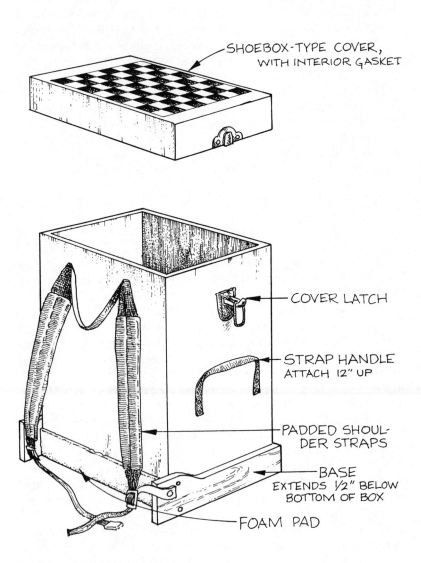

SHOEBOX-TYPE COVER,
WITH INTERIOR GASKET

COVER LATCH

STRAP HANDLE
ATTACH 12" UP

PADDED SHOUL-
DER STRAPS

BASE
EXTENDS 1/2" BELOW
BOTTOM OF BOX

FOAM PAD

Food pack.

Those versatile packs—a seat and *a checkerboard.*

of this, he gave it up as a lost cause and unceremoniously plunked the pack into the cold fireplace. Obviously chagrined at not gaining entry into the pack, his parting gesture was to clean off a shelf of cooking gear and utensils with one swipe of his huge paw. Without a backward glance, he lumbered away.

The Southers still have the pack. We replaced one ripped strap handle and re-bolted one shoulder strap. The tooth marks in the fiberglass are still there. To the Southers they are trophies of a memorable experience; to me they are a testimonial to the durability of my packs.

Construction

You can cut the parts for two food packs from one 4' x 8' sheet of ¼ inch plywood. (Cut the pieces as shown in the drawing of plywood parts.) The easiest way to cut these parts is on a table saw that is capable of a fence setting of at least 24 inches. If you lack a table saw, a local woodworking shop could do the whole thing in less than

Plywood parts for food packs. Use ¼" AD plywood—makes 2 packs.

fifteen minutes, and it shouldn't be too expensive. Once the ply-wood parts are cut, the rest of the job can be completed with hand tools.

If your latest remodeling project around the house left you with an extra sheet of paneling, there is no need to go out and buy plywood. Since most of the strength of these packs comes from the fiberglass, the quality of the wood is unimportant.

The plywood parts are easily assembled with a few ¾ inch brads and some white glue. I leave the brad heads above the surface and pull them when the glue dries, but they can be left in if you wish. All of the joints are simple butt joints, and the extra ½ inch or ¼ inch allowed in some of the dimensions indicates what butts against what.

When the glue is dry, round off and smooth up all edges and joints. This rounding off is important because if the fiberglass does

White wood glue is used to put the plywood pieces together. Here staples were used instead of brads.

not lie well over a sharp corner, you are apt to get bubbles. Do not round off the upper edge of the box or the lower edge of the cover: the fiberglass cloth is not brought over these edges, but is cut off flush with them. Keep the upper edge of the box flat and square so that it will seat well into the cover gasket you will install later.

I color code my boxes—each one is a different color. This way I can tell one from the other, and it saves a lot of searching when an item is needed. When I pack my meals I progress from lighter to darker colors. It might go like this: Breakfast meals—white box; lunches—yellow box; supper—red box. I also make note on my menu as to the boxes where I've packed extras like snacks, spare sugar, coffee, etc. Since these items would be at the bottom of the pack, this saves a lot of rummaging around.

The coloring process takes about five minutes and is very simple. Find any old (or new) paint of a suitable color. Thin it out (using paint thinner for oil-based paint or water for latex) until it is really runny, and apply the watered-down color to the plywood boxes with a rag or paint brush. Then smooth it out with a dry rag, just as if you were applying stain to a piece of furniture. The result of this home-made stain is a nice color of varied density due to the grain of the plywood. Even though it may seem to dry immediately, let it set overnight before you proceed with the fiberglass covering. If you like the idea of the checker/chess board on the cover, this is the time to paint it on.

Fiberglassing

The fiberglassing job will require about two quarts of polyester resin and four to five and one half yards of fiberglass cloth. I use six ounce cloth, but a heavier weight would be fine. I figured the cloth two ways—both based on a cloth width of 38 inches. If you are willing to use up pieces by overlapping, the smaller yardage will suffice. If you prefer to use entire sheets, then go with the longer piece. Fiberglass cloth *is* expensive, and I personally use up scrap pieces whenever I have them. The finished job is a little rougher, but not much, and with the beating and scratching these things take it hardly matters; their strength does not suffer.

Before fiberglassing, I glue one of my business cards to the box. When this is covered with cloth and resin it makes a permanent identification that is easily read through the clear fiberglass.

To get ready for fiberglassing, place each box and cover upside down on some sort of makeshift pedestal so that each is supported from the inside well above the work surface. This allows the fiber-

This box is being covered with one piece of 38" wide fiberglass cloth, but smaller, scrap pieces could be used without sacrificing strength or durability.

glass cloth to hang down over the edges; it will later be trimmed flush with the edges. If nothing is handy for a pedestal, let the box rest on narrow strips of wood, as we did in the photo.

Having draped the cloth over the box where you want it, mix the resin according to the instructions and start soaking the cloth with it, using a throw-away paint brush. Work from the center toward the edges and corners. Cut and fit the cloth as you come to the edges and corners with the resin. Don't try to do this fitting and cutting ahead of time—it just does not work out. The four corners of the boxes and covers are the hardest places to fit the cloth around; it is easy to end up with a gap here. For this reason, I always cut a small scrap piece to place over the initial layer at each corner. This doubling up ensures coverage and strength. Don't worry about rough edges at this point; still, do what you can to keep things as neat as possible. Use plenty of resin—all the cloth will hold without its running off.

If you can stay around while the resin is setting up, you should try to trim the cloth flush with the box and cover edges when the resin reaches the gel stage. (It will feel rubbery.) At this point it is easily trimmed flush with a sharp knife. Later, when the resin has completely cured, the trimming will take somewhat more effort.

After 24 hours or so, the boxes can be sanded. First smooth those rough spots where the cloth overlaps, then continue sanding the entire box to remove the glossy surface—this prepares it for the final coat of resin. Again, use as much resin as will hold without running off. If you sanded and feathered the edges of the overlapping fiberglass, the finished box will show no seams. However, if they show, no matter; this is a working box, not a piece of furniture.

You should probably give the insides of the boxes a couple of coats of varnish to seal the wood. Polyurethane varnish works well for this. (Be careful what you use. I once varnished a box with something—I don't know what—that turned out to smell terrible. The box still affects the taste of food left in it, so I use it as a tool pack.) It is good idea to delay the inside coating until all the fixtures are bolted in place, this way the varnish will help to seal and waterproof the holes.

Finishing

The bases on the boxes are built of pieces of ½ inch hardwood. These serve as skids to protect the bottom of the box. The base boards can be left straight or given a little shaping (as I did.) The important thing is that they extend ½ inch below the bottom of the box. They also extend ½ inch to the rear and about two inches to the front. My original idea was to stretch a strap across this two-inch extension; the strap was to rest against the small of the back when the box was being back-packed. I later found that pieces of closed-cell foam, such as ensolite, worked better than the strap, but I left the two-inch extension to protect the padding when the box is laid down—its usual position in the canoe. The half-inch extension to the rear and the skids on the bottom protect the fiberglass from the constant abrasion of rocks, sand and dirt.

Attach the bases with flathead stove bolts. Keep the countersunk heads inside the box so that the box sides will be smooth and snag-free. Trim the bolts flush with the nuts on the outside.

The ensolite is simply glued in place with contact cement. I use two thicknesses—just cement one layer right over the other.

The shoulder straps I use are the padded ones sold for pack frames. They usually come with their own mounting hardware; however, I prefer ¼-inch stove bolts to attach the upper end directly to the box. The lower (adjustable) end can be attached to the base with the clevis pins supplied with the straps. You can make your own straps with any available heavy piece of leather or webbing that is at least two inches wide. An army surplus store would be a good place to find inexpensive straps.

The strap handles can be made from any piece of webbing or leather ¾ inch to 1½ inch wide and about ten inches long. Attach them to the box with flathead stove bolts (keeping the flat head inside). Use washers between the nuts and the straps.

Once you have attached the strap handles and shoulder straps as shown in the drawing, you are ready to finish the cover.

The cover gasket is made from ordinary foam rubber weather stripping, available from most hardware stores. It is about ¼ inch thick and comes in various widths; use the ¾ inch width. Before applying it to the inside of the cover, make a channel for it by gluing strips of wood ¼ inch thick to the inside of the cover, ¾ inch from the cover lip. The rubber stripping is placed in the channel formed by the wood strips, and the tight fit plus the adhesive backing keep it in place. (Without the channel, the rubber would eventually roll or slide out of place.)

I don't want to give the impression that this gasket makes the box absolutely waterproof. It doesn't—if you hold a box underwater it will leak, but very slowly. However, the boxes have gone overboard in several canoe upsets, and in each case there was never enough water leakage to do any damage to the food. With the food packed in the box it will be heavier at the bottom, and the air space will make the box float with its top out of water. For the brief period the top portion may be underwater, the gaskets will keep out the water. To go to the trouble of *completely* waterproofing would be unnecessary, not to mention cumbersome and expensive.

The last items needed to complete the boxes are the cover latches (one on either side of each box). These are available at most hardware stores. Because of the shoe-box-style cover, you will have to build the lower unit of each latch up with a piece of wood so that it mates with the upper part. You'll need some help in getting these things located so that when completely installed they will pull the cover snug, with the top edge of the box pressing into the rubber gasket. Use some weight or bar clamps if you have them to pull the cover and box together and seat the gasket. Then proceed to carefully locate and drill the holes to attach the latches. Again, use flathead bolts, with the countersunk head inside the box and cover. The small wood screws that come with the latches are not satisfactory—use the stove bolts.

The bolt holes you have drilled in the box in attaching the various fixtures are probably well sealed by the tightened bolts. However, if you are worried about a possible leak, mix up a little resin and daub it on the bolts, nuts, and around the holes. You will also want to waterproof, with polyurethane or resin, the hardwood base of each box. This will help to seal the bolt holes in that area.

This finishes the boxes. I guarantee that they are rugged. You can sit on them, stand on them, drag them, drop them, let a bear play with them, and they will come through intact. Not indestructible, but close!

Materials

The following materials will be needed to construct a pair of food packs:

1 sheet (4' X 8') ¼ A-D plywood
1 small pack of ¾" brads
1 small bottle of white wood glue
Paint and thinner (for color stain)
4 to 5 ½ yards of 6 oz. (or heavier) fiberglass cloth
2 quarts of polyester resin
3 or 4 throw-away paint brushes
3 or 4 sheets of sandpaper (50 grit)
1 pint polyurethane varnish
4 pieces of hardwood, about ½" X 3" X 15" (dimension not critical)
48 flathead stove bolts, 1" long, with nuts
4 strap handles, plus hardware (or make your own)
4 trunk latches
10 feet of foam weather stripping, ¼" X ¾"
10 feet (linear) of wood strips, ¼" X ¾" (gasket channel)
2 bolts ¼" diam., 1" long for attaching shoulder straps at top—the straps usually come with clevis pins that can be used, to attach the lower ends to box bases)
4 strips of ensolite foam ½" X 3" X 15 ½" (can be cut from a short pad, with enough left over for future boxes)
2 pair of padded shoulder straps (or make your own)
1 small container of contact cement

The following tools will be needed to build the food packs:

Table saw
Hammer
Rule
Power sander (not a necessity)
Knife
Shears
Screwdriver
Hacksaw
Hand drill (electric or manual)
3/16" drill bit
¼" drill bit
Countersink
Pencil

Kitchen Pack

Riding crosswise in the middle of my twenty-foot canoe is the largest and heaviest pack on the trip—the kitchen pack. It makes an effective ballast to trim my canoe! If I have a light bow partner, I put it forward of the center thwart; with a heavier person it goes to the rear of it. It is a moderately heavy load to carry ashore, but wherever I set it down I have a complete kitchen.

The loaded box is not an unreasonable load for a portage on the back, and it is quite easy to get ashore using the strap handles. The point is, as long as the load is manageable, I would rather make one trip from canoe to campsite, or over a portage, than several trips with armloads of loose cooking gear. Another plus is that I can easily tuck in little goodies and luxuries that would be too much trouble otherwise.

My kitchen pack is not waterproof, as are the food packs, but there is little in it that would be ruined by a dunking. The few things that might be spoiled are relatively non-essential. The pack *is* rain proof, so there is no need to dash out and carry it to shelter when it rains. Like the other packs, it can remain outside, leaving the sheltered area for people instead of gear.

Design and Construction

The pack shown measures 19 inches by 30 inches by 8 ½ inches deep. You will want to make yours to accommodate your own equipment. I started out with a basic floor plan of my cookset, the plastic food containers, my Coleman stove, Coleman fuel, coffee

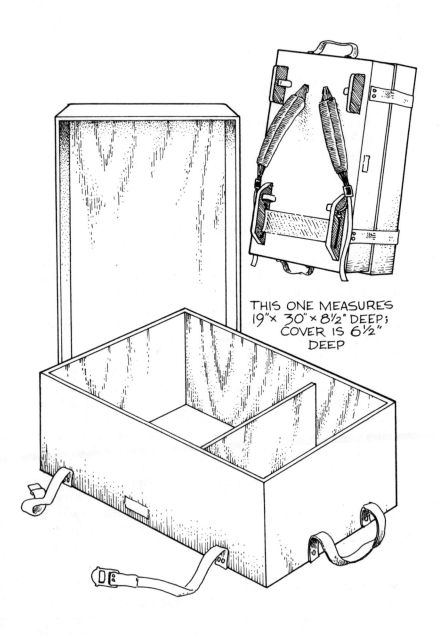

THIS ONE MEASURES
19"× 30"× 8½" DEEP;
COVER IS 6½"
DEEP

Kitchen pack—build to fit your gear.

pot, water pails, and the griddle standing at the end. The box was then designed to fit around these items. Everything else listed on the kitchen pack checklist is piled on top of these items or tucked in around them. When fully packed, everything is snug and fits tightly together.

The cover is of the shoe-box type, but much deeper than those on the food packs; mine is 6 ½ inches deep. This design allows the load in the box to vary—the cover sits high or low, depending on the load level, and keeps everything in place. The cover is secured by two canvas straps which, when fastened, can be used to lift the box as well as perform their primary function of holding the top down on the equipment. There are strap handles on each end, as well, for lifting the box.

There is a partition in my box between the cookset area and the Coleman stove. This is not a necessity but I find it useful when packing. I recommend you try it without a divider; it can easily be installed later if you feel it is needed.

The secret of the success of this kitchen pack, at least as far as I'm concerned, is its simplicity. No attempt was made to provide a separate compartment for every last item, and yet I could find any untensil in pitch dark because I always pack everything in the same arrangement. However, the pack easily allows any variations of equipment. I have used the same pack for many years without alterations and with minimum repairs. I think these facts speak well for its usefulness and versatility.

After you decide on the dimensions of your box, cut out the parts from ¼ inch plywood or a piece of surplus paneling. Assemble and fiberglass the box and its cover according to the directions for the food packs. (Don't forget to attach your name and address before fiberglassing if you want your pack to be permanently marked.)

The fixture attachment can be seen in the drawing. The blocks which serve as skids to protect the bottom from abrasion are designed to hold the pack about two inches off the ground. Make them of hardwood and attach them with wood screws from the inside of the box.

My pack still has a strap across the bottom skids to ease against the small of the back (when backpacking it). Someday, I will get around to replacing this with ensolite foam. Just as I have described in the instructions for the food packs, install the ensolite strips and the shoulder straps on the back of the pack.

The cover straps are attached to the lower edge of the box sides. They should be long enough to be fastened when the box is expanded to its maximum capacity. Install strap handles on each end to complete the fixtures on this simple pack.

When you design your kitchen pack, remember that the cover must slide down over the outside of the base. Make the *inside* dimension of the cover ½ inch *larger* than the *outside* dimension of the lower part (box) of the pack. This may seem like a lot to allow, but the box will be fiberglassed, and that will use part of this ½ inch allowance; besides, ½ inch means only ¼ inch on each side. The cover should slide easily up and down when completed.

The large flat surface of the cover is useful around the kitchen area. The smooth, easily cleaned surface is ideal for rolling out dough and for general food preparation, and the flat surface can be used for cooking and serving meals. The cover also makes an ideal windbreak for the campfire when I am trying to bake with the reflector oven on windy days. I just stand it on edge or on end and place a large rock on the lip, and the cover will stand there and allow

The kitchen pack cover being used as a windbreak for the reflector oven.

the biscuits to bake as well as they would on a nice calm day.

Mine isn't, but your cover could be, painted with a game board of your choice. However, it makes a good card table, as is, and guests have used it many times while waiting out the wind or other disagreeable weather.

Make your kitchen pack to meet your own needs and to fit your equipment. If you have ideas of your own by all means work them in, but the best advice I can give is, keep it simple. Simplicity means versatility!

Materials

The following materials will build your kitchen pack. The tools necessary to do the job are the same as those listed for constructing the food packs.

1 sheet (4 ' X 8') ¼" A-D grade plywood (more than enough)
2 yards of 6 oz. (or heavier) fiberglass cloth
1 quart of polyester resin
1 small pack of ¾" brads
1 small bottle of white glue
Some paint and thinner (for color stain, if desired)
2 or 3 throw-away brushes
2 or 3 sheets of sandpaper (50 grit)
1 pint polyurethane varnish
1 piece of hardwood, ¾" X 2" X 24" (to make bottom skids)
24 ¾" No. 8 flathead wood screws (to attach skids)
4 pieces of canvas strap with 2 buckles (cover hold-down)
8 flathead stove bolts, 1" long, with nuts
2 ½" bolts, 1" long (for attaching shoulder straps)
2 strips of ensolite ½" X 3" X 16"
1 small container of contact cement
2 strap handles, plus hardware (or make your own)

Pack Frame

Unlike the rest of my custom gear, which came about from necessity, the pack frame was a spin-off. After learning the ins and outs and dos and don'ts of bending wood for snowshoes, I started looking around for other ways to use my new-found skills. The pack frame was one of the things I tried. I didn't really expect anything special, but thought it would be nice to use a self-made pack, anyway.

The aluminum frames I had always used had given pretty good service, I thought. But the abuse of hefting them in and out of canoes in summer and loading them on and off snowmobile sleds in winter (plus any other rough treatment they received) caused bends where they were not supposed to be and even some broken welds at the joints. As a matter of course, I planned to replace them every two or three years, and expected to do the same with the wooden pack frame I built.

The satisfaction of using self-made equipment was motive enough for me to use the pack frame, but after a couple of years went by I was discussing the frame with someone, and I realized how long I had been using it. I looked it over closely and was surprised to find no signs of wear, breaks, bends, or any of the other problems I had come to expect with metal frames.

The reason the wood frame had held up so well was its flexibility. It was designed to have the rigidity to do the job, yet be flexible enough to give and yield to rough handling. This ability to give is partly due to the inherent quality of the wood and partly due to the nylon-wrapped joints. (This is the only fastening method used throughout the construction.) My own frame is now in its fifth year of constant use, and is still going strong. I couldn't be happier with it!

You can build two versions of the wood pack frame—one caned, and one cross-braced and padded. (See the photographs.)

Bending the Wood

The wood I use for building pack frames is the same as I use for snowshoes—white ash. I confess I have never used any other wood, but if ash were unavailable I am sure I could find many other hardwoods that would work. Ash has the happy combination of hardness, strength, and light weight, and it bends well. Whatever kind of wood you use, be sure it is straight-grained and free of knots or other imperfections.

All frame parts should be cut a couple of inches longer than the dimensions shown in the drawing. This allows for the bending; any excess can be trimmed off to exact dimensions when the pack is assembled. Cut two uprights about 37 inches long from ¾" × 1 ¼" stock for the caned model and ¾" × ¾" stock for the uncaned version. (The extra width of the uprights in the caned model is to allow for the holes that must be drilled for the cane.) Cut four cross bars about 16 inches long from ⅜" × 1 ½" stock.

The secret of bending wood is to saturate it with lots of moist heat. For this project, moist heat can best be supplied by boiling

The wood pack frame—tough and resilient. This uncaned model uses two angular rope braces in the center section to keep the frame square.

water in some kind of container long enough to submerge all of the hardwood pieces. If you plan to use steam rather than boiling water, you should pre-soak the wood for several hours to be sure it is good and wet. Boiling or steaming should go on for at least two hours.

Custom Gear 137

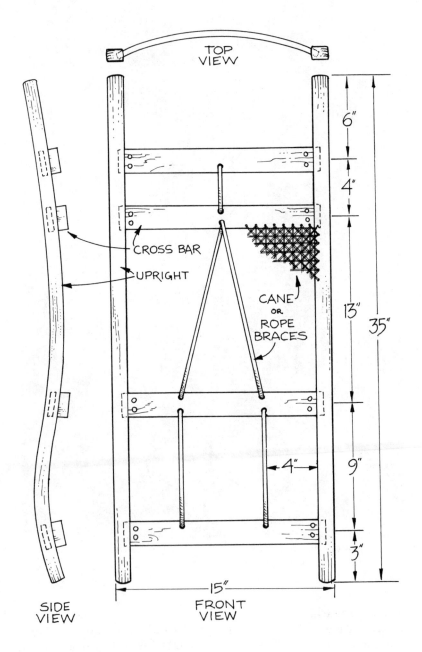

TOP
VIEW

6"

4"

CROSS BAR

UPRIGHT

CANE
OR
ROPE
BRACES

13"

35"

4"

9"

3"

15"

SIDE
VIEW

FRONT
VIEW

Wood pack frame.

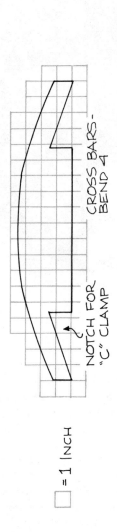

CROSS BARS-
BEND 4

NOTCH FOR
"C" CLAMP

MAKE FROM 2" X 4"s

= 1 INCH

ARROWS INDICATE POSITIONS OF CROSSBAR MORTISES
IN FINISHED FRAME

UPRIGHTS - BEND 2

NOTCH FOR
"C" CLAMP

Pack frame bending forms.

Simple forms and "C" clamps are used to bend the hot wood.

The wood must be hot all the way through.

The frame parts are bent over the forms shown in the scaled drawing. Make the forms for the cross bars from pieces of two-by-four. (You should have four of these forms so the job can all be done at one time.) The form for the uprights should be thick enough in breadth so that the pieces can be laid on it side by side for bending. You could make it by cutting out two pieces from two-by-four stock and then gluing or nailing them together.

You will want five or six "C" clamps for bending and holding the wood on the forms. For the cross bars, use the clamps to draw the material down over the form and then wrap the ends with wire or rope so that the clamps can be removed and used for the next cross bar. (Of course, if you have plenty of clamps, then simply leave them in place.) Clamps with a three-inch opening are all right for bending the cross pieces. The uprights will require larger clamps; I

use those with a six-inch opening. (plan on at least three of these.) Leave the clamps in position on the uprights until the wood is ready to remove from the form. Before you begin the bending process, have some scraps of wood handy to place between the clamps and the hot wood, for the wood is soft in this condition and dents easily.

Work as fast as possible. An assistant is helpful but not absolutely necessary. The idea is to get the hot wood bent into the desired shape before it has a chance to cool off. Once the wood is bent over the forms and is secured in place, set it all aside to dry. The amount of time required for drying will vary with humidity and temperature, but play it safe—leave it at least a week in a dry warm area. Don't forget to mark your uprights for the cross bar mortises before you remove them from the form.

Assembly
Before the pack frame can be assembled, the mortises for the

cross bars must be cut into the uprights. The mortises should be just under 1½ inches long by ¼ inch wide by 5/16 to ⅜ inch deep. No, this isn't large enough to accommodate the ⅜ by 1½ inch cross bar, but it is easier to cut the mortises to a standard dimension—a little small, then trim the end of the cross bar for a good fit.

A look at the detail drawing of the pack frame shows that the mortise must be cut at an angle to accept the curved cross bar and still keep everything somewhat flat and plumb. I never get too scientific about this angle because it isn't too critical. The important thing is that all eight of the mortises be nearly the same. I found that by shimming the upright in a vise with a couple of wedges cut to 12 degrees would allow me to cut a vertical mortise. When removed from the vise, the mortise would be angled in the upright. Hold your cross bar up to the upright and you can see the necessary angle clearly. Be *very careful* to cut the angle in the right direction. Check

Cutting mortises with a drill press router. The blocks of wood in the vice are cut at 12 degrees so the router bit enters the upright at the proper angle. The same devices would work for hand cutting.

and double check. It may be a mental block with me, but I have had to remake uprights because I somehow got the cussed angle going the wrong way.

If you have a router or mortise cutter, use them, of course, but a few minutes' work with a hammer and a ¼ inch wood chisel will do the trick just as well.

When all eight mortises have been cut, trim your cross bars so that the overall (outside) width of the frame is what you desire. Mine is 15 inches, I think this is standard for most bags, although wider ones are available. Check your bag. Be sure to allow for the depth of your mortise in determining the length of the cross bar. To keep the curve even, measure each way from the cross bar center and trim both ends to length.

Trim the ends of the cross bars so that they fit snugly into the mortises. I mean *snug, not tight*; if you have to drive them in, you are apt to split the upright. Strive for a good wood-to-wood contact the entire depth of the mortise.

When all cross bars are fitted, put the frame together. The best way to hold everything securely in place while you permanently fasten it is to wrap a small rope around the assembled frame near each end, tie them, then twist with a stick to pull the uprights together until everything lines up and the cross bars are secure in their mortises. Be sure that the cross bars are square with the uprights before proceeding with assembly.

The cross bars and uprights are held together by wrapping with nylon mason's line, which is available from most hardware stores. Using a ¼ inch bit, drill two holes on each end of the cross bars, about ½ inch from the upright. The nylon line is passed through these holes and around the outside of the uprights. With a little care, a nice neat job can be made of it. Keep the line even and neatly laid side by side around the upright. Twelve wraps, six in each hole, is about right. Keep the line as tight as possible as you wrap, and tie off in an inconspicuous place. Melt the end of the nylon so it will not slip through. Keep checking your frame with a square as you secure the eight cross bar ends.

The nylon rope braces are made with the same nylon line as is used for wrapping. Drill ¼ inch holes in the crossbars (as shown in the drawing), about ½ inch in from the edge, and thread the line through six or eight times for each brace. You could, instead of drilling the holes, just go around the cross bar. Either way, keep the line taut as you work, but not tight. If you attempt to pull the line too tight, the cross bars will be bent and pulled toward one another.

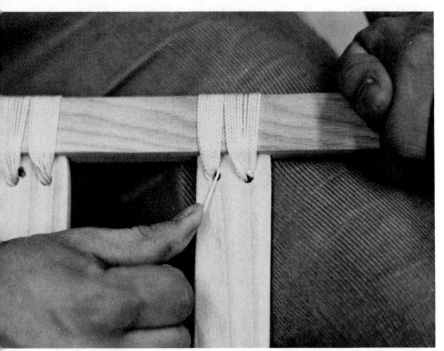

Making one of those flexible joints. The nylon is thoroughly soaked with polyurethane when the frame is complete.

After you have made the six or eight trips around, wrap the bundle of lines with the same line so that you end up with one solid rope, or so it appears. You can tie the line off by passing the end through the last loop in the wrap and melting the end. If you are making the caned model you will have one short brace on top and two longer ones at the bottom. If you do not plan to cane the center section, make two long angular braces to hold the frame square. These braces are made in the same way as the others, except that you will need a larger hole where the two come together (unless you go around the cross bar).

If you are making the uncaned model, finish it at this point with three coats of polyurethane varnish. When you put on the first coat, be sure to *thoroughly* soak the nylon wraps and braces. Make them absorb all of the varnish they can. This is what gives them their stability and abrasion resistance.

The caning requires a series of holes all the way around the area to be covered; you'll drill ¼ inch holes on a line ⅜ inch from the inside edge all the way around the opening. When marking the locations of the holes, space them ¾ inch apart, and start from the center of each side to ensure that the holes on each side are opposite their counterparts on the other side. (This should not be a problem since the space is a rectangle, but working outward from the center of each side will show up possible mistakes for correction before drilling.) When the cane holes are drilled, go ahead and put on the polyurethane varnish as previously described.

Caning

It is not within the scope of this book to offer a course in caning. It is not a difficult thing to learn, and there are some good references which offer step-by-step instructions. I first learned caning so that I could install caned seats in the strip canoes we were building. I

Making a caned model. Real class!

obtained a copy of Cornell Extension Bulletin 681, *Cane Seats for Chairs* by Ruth Comstock, from my county extension office. It was free. The step-by-step photos are easy to follow. If it is unavailable locally, this bulletin can be obtained for a fee from the University at Ithaca, New York.

You should be able to find instructional material *and* cane at hobby or craft stores. If the cane is not available locally, pick up a craft magazine and check the ads. I recommend the plastic cane for outdoor use rather than the natural cane, which will permanently sag when damp.

As you proceed with the caning, be sure the frame remains square. This cane replaces the angular (middle) braces, and it does a good job of it, but you *must* keep everything square until the job is complete.

The caning job serves some important functions: it replaces the pad you'd otherwise install to rest against the mid-back, it holds the frame square, and it acts as part of the firm yet flexible binding of the frame. But, all these practical advantages aside, it gives the frame *real class!* I highly recommend it.

Attaching the Fixtures

The fixtures you will need to complete the pack are: a bag, padded shoulder straps, and a pad for the lower back. If you make the uncaned model, you will also need a pad for the mid-back. All of these, along with the necessary attaching hardware, are available from outdoor stores that cater to backpackers. (I use a padded hip belt for the lower back pad, but this is up to you.)

Attach the fixtures according to manufacturer's directions or, lacking these, the way the manufacturer attaches them to the completed units in the store or catalog.

Don't expect yowls of enthusiasm from your backpacking friends over your new pack. It is probably a few ounces heavier than the lightweight tubular aluminum jobs, and this difference is important to folks who cut off tooth brush handles to save weight; however, for the rough handling of day in, day out canoe tripping it is the best there is. No doubt about it!

Materials

You will need the following materials to build your pack frame:

2 pieces of ash ¾″ X 1¼″ X 37″ (can be ¾″ X ¾″ X 37″ for the uncaned model)

4 pieces of ash ⅜" X 1½" X 16"
1 roll of nylon mason's line
4 pieces of 2 X 4, 17" long (bending forms, cross bars)
2 pieces of 2 X 4, 38" long (bending forms, uprights)
1 pint polyurethane varnish
1 hank of medium plastic cane (for caned model only)
Fixtures
1 pack bag
1 pair of padded shoulder straps
1 pad (or padded hip belt) for lower back
1 pad or wide band for upper back (for uncaned model)

The following tools will be needed for pack frame construction:

Table saw
2 "C" clamps, 3" opening (could use more if available)
3 "C" clamps, 6" opening
Router or ¼" wood chisel to cut mortises
Hammer
Pencil
Hand drill, electric or manual
¼" drill bit
Rule
Framing square
Container long enough to boil the 37" uprights, or a steamer
Source of heat for steamer or boiler

8 Back-paddle

Years of teaching in a high school vocational shop have had the result of causing me to give instructions in minute, sometimes even painful, detail. I have had to keep reminding myself throughout this book that it was not being written for the beginning canoeist—that I did not have to start out from the bottom in all cases. Yet, I wanted enough information for those persons preparing for their first trip with responsibilities beyond themselves.

I hope that the experienced old-timer will find hints, tips and methods that can be used and improved upon. Some river guides reading this will say, "That son-of-a-gun got that idea from me." Guilty! I have never said everything was original. It would take considerable space to give them all credit, and besides, some of them I met briefly on the river, and never did learn their names.

If you are an accomplished white water canoeist, you may feel I do not give my people enough instruction in the sport. Time is the controlling factor: In a period of 7 to 10 days I have to get these people down a hundred miles or so of river, *besides* instructing them. So, practice *and* instruction have to be accomplished while we're underway. If I am fortunate enough to have people with canoeing experience, then I can go into more advanced skills like eddy turns, setting, the ferry, and all the other nice-to-know things about canoe handling in white water.

I am proud of my equipment, both store-bought and self-made. It fits my operation and has stood the test of time. Next year I will add a new, long-handled, heavy duty, stainless steel spatula; that's an indication of the point I have reached as far as equipment changes are concerned. I hope you will find some of my items of custom gear useful and adaptable to your own outfit.

Good canoeing!

Index